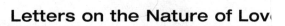

Letters on the Nature of Love

Letters on the Nature of Love

Janet Braithwaite

YOUCAXTON PUBLICATIONS

Contents

List of Drawings

Frontispiece - etching and aquatint.
Portrait of Cees Landsaat reading a love poem by the
Greek Alexandrian poet Constantine Cavafy.

FRAGMENTS FROM
A FAR-OFF FRACTURED TIME
GREECE, 1961-1965

Agamemnon[1]

Once on a dusty road from Thebes
Agamemnon stopped his lorry
and slouched forward wearily
slung across the steering wheel
in momentary sleep

raising a face
lined and hollow
released from the angular confines
of a golden mask

eyes deep and dark
staring out
across the centuries
all – seeing.

Pou pas, koritsi mou?[2]

Perhaps a lift?
In a lorry
driven by a legend
far older than history
half asleep at the wheel?

Agamemnon
wandering on the plain of Thebes
far from the massive ruins
of Mycenae.

Aborted

Slats of sunlight carved upon consciousness
awareness of groaning and pain
disembodied.
A voice blurred by distance
breaking through the darkness
dark prison walls
and hands
powerless to thrust open weighted eyelids
imprisoned tears
an unknown place
and hands
shadowed on the darkness.
And yet these slats of light
upon my shuttered eyes
or lines upon a shirt
a face forming around the distant voice
my body taking shape around its groaning breath.

Outside the sun is shining –
unbelievably.
We return to an accustomed rhythm
resurrected
to intensity of happiness
reborn innocence
but no – an anaesthetic
delaying the birth of horror and revulsion
out of mutilation
the core of love hacked as yet but from the body
shattered and twisted
and the mind, drugged, unaware,
watches its stumbling dreams fall
into the bleeding wound
and, drown,
powerless

And yet they say
that ghosts claim burial.
We should have known
a child's ghost would torture us,
but not for burial
but not for burial
for light denied.
And yet they say
that sin is merely this,
the unforgivable transgression,
to violate the natural growth of things
to their fulfilment,
interrupting fate.
How could we then believe we would not die
our hearts' own death?
Resentful ghosts
staring in hostility
across a stream of bitterness.
And yet our eyes are weeping.

Greek Tragedy with Modern Sequel

She lost her way wandering within the confused maze
between the letter of the law and dictates of the heart
that to be happy she must keep the child unconditionally,
not deny it light nor sacrifice her body to the knife
of some legal doctor butchering illegal merchandise

in the clean white sterile clinic, nor sacrifice her body
to custom and the cowardice of love which fails to stand
against the pressures of the current. But stricken she gave in.
She woke to the quiet weeping of women in the clean white sterile clinic
where grief and sin pollute with contagion of secret disease.

Relieved, he took her home. But madness shrieked within her: "what fools
to think we could survive intact, unhaunted and unharmed,
trusting love's fragility to withstand nightmares, loaded down
with memories that will not fade of the clean white sterile clinic
of some legal doctor butchering illegal merchandise".

Wandering in the mind's crazed maze where law is powerless
to hold back the unleashed furies of madness and of grief
she wrought havoc, destroyed whatever else remained
and fled from the man she had loved and that foreign city
where grief and sin pollute with contagion of secret disease.

Time passed, but she stayed still corroded into rituals
of endless expiation, and yet found the grace of loving.
Longing for acceptance at last she risked her guilty secret.
"You shouldn't have told me that", he said. "I'm a good punisher".
And she froze. But beyond the prick of usual tears a blaze

of unsuspected anger burst as, sated with suffering, she
put an end to penance inwardly: outwardly docile
to his threats of cruelty she waited in wonder at day dreams
of violence, of triumphant revenge shattering through her pain
as wild music breaks tumultuous through the sadness of her days.

After the peaceful walk in the country he sat in her car,
poised for the kill. "We're through. I've found someone more interesting".
he said, casually brutal, outlined against the setting sun.
"Daughter of a prostitute and a better screw than you".
And she froze. But beyond the prick of usual tears, ablaze,

she steadied, pressed down her foot, sent the car downhill at breakneck
speed, grazed through the tightening gap between the bus and the brick wall.
She took him home, left him scared shitless, shaking on the pavement
as wild music breaks tumultuous through the sadness of her days
when lost she used to wander within the confused maze.

Structure of Tragedy

For Menelaos Daphlos, actor, teacher and superb dancer.

One night
we faced across a crowded table
dazed by the cry of music in an enclosed room.
In those few hours
I broke my prison bars
and rushed to meet you
through the frontier lines of our resisting loneliness
in that elusive no-man's land of alien intimacy
where, enforced conscripts of our nationalities,
we put off our armour,
threw our weapons down
and with a joyful cry of recognition,
defenceless,
ran to clasp each other,
living our naked legend
beyond constraints of time and attitude.

The words of Pylades [3], talking quietly in a café:
"No doubt, there is no doubt she loves you,
but what is that
if she would not share your life with you?"
words overheard by chance, hard, irrefutable,
crushing the fragile flowering of our timelessness.
Practical Pylades, who loved us both
and knew us better than ourselves.
And when we danced, intense and beautiful,
those who sat in the cafés looking on
envied our beauty and our happiness;
but he alone,
watching the intricate figures of our grief,
admired and pitied us.

Departure – and you left behind
a silence
unwounded by uncomprehending words
an order
unlivened by spasmodic strife of hope against despair
a loneliness
untroubled by the painful yearn of eyes
to pierce each others' deep illegibility
the vain attempt of hands
to still each others' trembling
travelling down through knotted veins
from the dark pulse of panic and despair.
And lying here
as in the silent bareness of a clinic room,
which waits upon its occupant's slow death,
measuring the steady passing of the hours
by the quiet fall of automatic tears
your words pound in my ears like heart beats
curbing with their steady tread
the hysteric rise of pain.
"Fate in fact is nothing more than time."

Greece from a Long Perspective.

Greece

     was my bi-polar paradise
     my native land of wild extremes
     familiar to my soul's
     ecstatic yearnings for intensity –
     apotheosis of my dreams.

Greece

     so ancient and so mythical
     possessed by gods
     yet so vibrant and alive
     so passionately present;
     so earthboundly human, so paganly divine.

Greece

     with its bleached, sun-baked plains
     silvered by shimmering olives
     slashed by shadows dark as iron
     where glimpsed ghosts march forever
     - soldiers old as Thermopylae [4]
     shoulder to shoulder through the snow
     with recent comrades dead
     hardly eighty years ago [5]
     in war's futile lunacy,
     their names still clearly legible
     carved on dark pines in northern forests
     where grey wolves roam merging into shadow.

A walk across a mountainside –
a long day's walk
austere and lonely
far from any place –
I am so utterly alone.
When suddenly
from behind a rock
steps out Apollo
young and radiant
crowned with golden curls
burnished by the sun.

"Xeni isai? Apo pou?
Ti kanis etho moni sou sta vouna?"
"Anglitha imai. Taxidevo sta pothya makria sta vouna.
M'aresi i monaxya. Pos se leni?"[6]
We asked simple questions,
curious to know.
Elemental children
at the dawn of time.

He offered me erota[7]
unbuttoning his trouser front
to make his meaning clear.
I thanked him
but declined his precious gift,
unready and unsure.
He did not persist.
We parted
on the mountainside
- I walked on alone -
elemental children
at the dawn of time.

Beware! -
the gods are beautiful
the gods are passionate
playful and petulant
and full of mischievous caprice.

Beware! -
the gods are dangerous
the gods are immortal
vengeful, jealous, irascible,
implacable and full of power.

"Those whom they would destroy
they first make mad."[8]

Dazzled by the brilliance
lightning – struck
I lost my way
condemned to wander
all directionless
unmapped
utterly astray.

Greece
where I found myself
then lost myself again.

Paradise, once lost,
can never be regained.
Its wild, ecstatic loveliness survives
within the passionate interstices
of memory,
lit by the distant glow
of that reflected, far off, fervent brilliance
unsubdued by age or time or pain.

Notes

1   Agamemnon was an ancient king living at the margins of time where history merges with legend. He was king of the rich and powerful city of Mycenae in the Peloponnese of which the ruins still exist. Mycenae was at the height of its power between 1400 and 1200 BC and Agamemnon probably ruled towards the end of this period. Nine gold masks were excavated in shaft tombs in the city, one of which was almost certainly the death mask of Agamemnon. He fought in the Trojan War in support of his brother, Menelaos, king of Sparta, whose wife, Helen, had run away with Paris to Troy where his father was king. Later Agamemnon was murdered by his wife, Clytemnestra, who took power and ruled with her lover, Aegisthos. Their son, Orestes, who was still a child when his father was murdered, fled to a neighbouring kingdom, and was given refuge by the king and befriended by the king's son, Pylades. When he grew to manhood Orestes was fated to kill his mother, as it was considered the duty of a son to avenge a murdered father.

2   Where are you going, my girl?

3   Pylades was the life-long friend of Orestes, who accompanied him during his years of exile and shared the tribulations of his life and his journeys as he fled from the Furies, goddesses who took revenge on matricides, after he killed his mother to avenge the murder by her of his father. After many years of harassment both men were eventually allowed by the gods to marry and lead peaceful lives. Pylades became the by-word for loyalty and all-enduring friendship faithful until death.

4   The battle of Thermopylae took place in BC 480 when the combined forces of Greece led by Athens and Sparta failed to hold the narrow mountain pass of Thermopylae against the Persian army, led by their king, Xerxes, in spite of the heroic stand by 300 Spartan soldiers under their leader, Leonidas, who held the pass against overwhelming numbers until they were wiped out. This was an unmitigated disaster leading to the evacuation and fall of Athens and leaving the whole of Southern Greece open to invasion by the Persian army, then the most feared and powerful military force in the Mediterranean world whose elite core were known as the Immortals. Athens, which was the leading maritime power in Greece and beyond, managed to use its fleet to evacuate the entire population of the city and take them to safety. The situation was reversed later in the year at the battle of Salamis when the Athenian fleet decisively defeated the Persian fleet which was off the Greek coast in support of their army, and Xerxes decided to retreat and take his army back to Asia Minor.

5   This refers to the 2nd World War when German and Italian armies marched through Greece laying waste to the north in particular, immediately followed by a bitter and bloody civil war between the forces supporting the royal family and the right-wing government and the communists, during which Northern Greece suffered particularly badly again.

6   "Are you a foreigner? Where are you from? What are you doing here all alone on the mountains?"

"I'm English. I'm travelling on foot far over the mountains. I like loneliness. What is your name?"

I use the Greek to try and catch the lively curiosity of all Greeks and especially Greeks living in the isolated, mountainous areas of mainland Greece at that time, where they hardly ever met foreigners. They asked very direct, unselfconscious questions and were so passionately interested to know where you were from, what it was like in your country, what you were doing in Greece, what it was like in Europe which they didn't feel they belonged to at all at that time.

7   Greek has two words for "love":-"agapi" meaning "love" in English and "Eros, erota" which has no exact equivalent in English, encompassing as it does the bodily delight and pleasure of sexual love and the ecstasy of the mind, and even spirit, in the intensity of love and physical union. Eros is, after all, a god and a youthful and mischievous one at that, being somewhat similar to Puck as portrayed in "A Midsummer Night's Dream" but far more powerful.

8   Verse 620-623 from Sophocles "Antigone"

LETTERS ON THE NATURE OF LOVE
1990-1991

Letters on the Nature of Love

For years I've been writing
secret letters from the battlefield
on the nature of love.
Usually they are in code
or more often
knowing no one will understand
they're never written down at all
just held in mind.

But here they are at last
in the open
written out
entrusted
to your integrity.

Declarations of Difference

I would do most things for you
even serving in the rearguard
which isn't my natural position,
God knows, preferring as I do
the front line and the heroic journey
where you can see what you're at
- the subtle terrors of the rearguard
 are not my cup of tea
- all those insidious deceits
 the darkness darts at us to drag us down
- but anything for you – well, almost anything.

But don't ask me to be less vulnerable.
Vulnerability is my element
- I swim in it more surely
 as the years go by
- it's what I'm good at.
Given the choice
I probably wouldn't have chosen
 to be high tension cable
- I'd probably have gone for
something more comfortable
given the choice.
But as things are you might as well
ask the river not to be wet.

Vulnerability isn't what you fear
- being lured to deflection from chosen desire paths
too passively bruised by others' harsh realities
too pliantly taking the print of inauthentic pain.

Vulnerability is being
 there at the furthest edges of intensity
 where pain and joy blur and there's only energy
- soundless music -
 where I am the strings trembling in harmony
 vibrant with the moment's ecstasy
- instrumental -
 but the music
 shimmering through my fragile resonance
- the music is eternal.

The Morning After the Night Before

The night he left
life took over pretty quickly.
When I got home
there were four drunks
strewn about on the pavement
outside my gate
eating mega-pizzas.
On closer inspection
one of them turned out to be my son
except that he wasn't really drunk –
in fact, I have to admit,
I was quite proud of him
- although it didn't show much at the time -
being the only one
in any kind of control of himself
and the youngest by at least two years.
So having seen he could sort out the situation
I went to bed.

I didn't know how I would feel in the morning
but I woke up
feeling bloody marvellous
rested from battle
light of heart
as you might expect, I suppose,
of a soldier of the line
after a successful engagement
especially in the rearguard
where the fighting's trickiest.
Life being what it is
I've got used to the cut and thrust
of the front line
but serving in the rearguard
calls for nerves of steel
ready to respond
to ambush, treachery
all those insidious deceits
the darkness darts at us
to drag us down.

So when I had to walk into the classroom
all unprepared
to give a class on idioms
I didn't mind at all
writing nonchalantly on the board
the first thing that came into my head
'burning the candle at both ends',
'holding the fort'
and going on from there.
As usual –
metaphor having a life of its own –
it soon took over,
slithering across the interface
between realities
where language melts
and loses its coherent frame,
words slip liquidly
volatile
streaming
quicksilver.

Duality

I am that most unfashionable creature,
the womanly woman
- doubly so -
with the extremely male animus figure.
As a result we've had lots of problems
he and I.
For years he languished in prison
while I was weak and sick at heart
but since he managed to break out
we've both been a lot happier.
He's never really been keen on
hanging about on the fringes
of feminist meetings
according to present fashion
preferring to range through time sword in hand
fighting battles mostly on the side of the light
well – there have been the odd confusions
we've both occasionally got into bad company
just for a short time.
As a matter of fact I'm not crazy
about assertiveness training either –
saxophone players tend not to have that particular problem.

Journey

I stand there
crucified across the axis of your parting
feeling the anchor tearing through my soul
sadness of harbours slashed by the cries of seabirds
desolation
panic in my throat
rending
fibres parting
rending
rending.

But then the moment passes – only a moment -
knife flash as our bodies move apart.
Receding
I move back
reintegrating
ebbing
calm
entrusting you to time.

Struggling for Words

I'm gazing steadily into your eyes
watching the signs
alert to danger threatening

'Don't be so vulnerable'.

Suddenly some dark floodgate of terror starts to move.
Panic rises, choking dark inchoate.
I've got to say something, put some name between it and me
- the containing power of words
making the unknowable known friendly familiar -
before it reaches my throat
and I'm strangled
overwhelmed.

Somewhere in time
I'm fighting for survival
on some dark field
nerves taut and alert
in total concentration
shield to shield
as the line threatens to break
knowing the totality of annihilation
you know it too – I can see the fear in your eyes
that waits there
if my glance drops now we're lost
when one man falls
and the line breaks
gazing steadily into your eyes
if my glance slips away now we're lost
holding the centre calm through the mirror of our eyes
and somewhere in time
the line holds.

'Does it frighten you?'
'A bit'
- the benediction of words.
I want to say, 'don't worry
you're just misinterpreting the signs
it's only a problem of translation'
but as usual
I can't find the words.

Cross-cultural Celebrations

When you come home
we'll hang out the flags
- well, maybe not the flags
we might have difficulty deciding which ones
and end up arguing. Who needs flags anyway!? –
paint the town red
bang the drums
blow the saxophones
kill the fatted calf
roll out the barrel
- none of that should cause us any problems -
pop the champagne corks
and dance all night.
Come to think of it – I've never seen you dancing
well, never mind – I can dance enough for two
while you occasionally catch my hand
and prop up the bar – or I might try teaching you
- it's about time you learnt the gentler arts -
and anyway dancing can't be that different from football.

Apprenticeship on the Bi-polar Spectrum

I have spent many years
learning to stand
where the planes of the axis cross.
Of course it's dangerous
standing there
naked and alone
bracing body and mind
to take the lightening flash
submitting to the current's flow
praying that the tension holds.
But I am strong and brave
tempered in fire
tested on the threshold of death
resilient
training myself more willingly
as the years pass by
growing more confident
in skills acquired
intuitively
self-taught
by listening in the silence
to the inner pulse of being
walking in the darkness
through territory
where the paths are no longer mapped,
the rituals forgotten, ridiculed.
You could call it my vocation.

I admit
there are times
when I long for a companion
- there at the axis
where the planes cross
it's so lonely -
a comrade at arms
strong and brave enough
to stand shoulder to shoulder
laughing at danger
willing to share
the wildness
of desperation
of exhilaration
there where the planes cross
and the structure holds
separating light from darkness.

So I wait here
trusting the signs
the power of talismans
the prophecies of dreams.

OF FAMILY, FRIENDS
AND MUCH LOVED PLACES

A Death in the Family

In loving memory of my brother, Bob Beech, who died all too young

The first time it happened we were sitting in my place
watching the sun glint through the rows of trees round the Catholic
graveyard and idly discussing what to do with the boat
and which of the Birmingham pubs had the best gigs for jazz.
When he decided to go he couldn't get on his feet.
I could see his youngest was unsure whether to laugh or cry.

I have to admit it was funny as he collapsed
on the couch. I snatched the phone, "my brother's having a stroke,
I think. Can you come right away" and shepherded the kids
 into the gravity-defying wreckage of the front room
- I was decorating at the time – flung a few pieces
of furniture out of the way as the doctor turned up,

followed by the ambulance. The tall bookcase leaning
at a crazy angle chose that exact moment to fall
knocking over a bucket of water and burying
the screaming kids under a deluge of books and its frame,
the doctor and the men let my brother slip from their hands
to the floor, the wheelchair jammed in the passage which would aspire

to be a hall, and the whole bloody world keeled over leaning
drunken and shipwrecked with all hands overboard, all hands
lost, as his broken body was wheeled out and lifted up
into the ambulance. I quickly dusted down the kids
and franticly attempted to pick up the pieces
of my household, then phoned my sister-in-law at her workplace

- that's how trouble started, him marrying a Catholic.
No – he was always defiant, always seemed to aspire
to being the naughtiest boy in class, would never cry
when he was in trouble, insisted on listening to jazz.
When he returned home fully recovered from the stroke
sometimes we'd remember the look on the doctor's face and fall

about laughing. Things eased between us with him back on his feet.
We seemed closer than we'd been for years, though still burying
the bitter taste of rows in filtered talk, denying room
to certain quarrelsome words. Perhaps we sensed the whole frame-
work of our lives was shifting as blood pressed in tight veins collapsed
the tissues and thrusting grasses stressed the structure of the boat.

31

That was one of our best times together – building the boat,
excitedly watching it take shape under our hands,
unskilled and often hammered as they stretched stringers round its frame,
totally united against the parental ban on jazz.
Mum and Dad, though generally liberal, were hardly catholic
in their tastes in music. He always took the most exposed place,

fearless in the face of Dad's fury, even when we were kids,
always in the forefront. I admired but didn't aspire
to more than the rearguard. There's a snap of him blackberrying
- he 'd have been about six – with an insolent grin looking up
at m' Dad who's laying down the law – awesome even in defeat.
Then one day without warning he suddenly collapsed

at work. He never really recovered from the second stroke.
When he came out of hospital his mouth was leaning
crookedly to one side, as if trying to force out a cry
frozen on his lips. His paralysed right side let fall
his useless hand. His shattered life shrank into a single room.
My sister-in-law steadfastly began to pick up the pieces.

Mum secretly didn't like him marrying a Catholic.
She told me but not him. I've no time for all that jazz
with God, being agnostic with an atheistic leaning.
Never understood why death-bed repentees could catch the boat
after life-times of cheerful sinning, whereas there was no room
for decent gods-fearing pagans. I tried to stop the fall –

out. "For Chrissake, is it really that important?" and got put in my place
for blaspheming. My sister-in-law, having picked up
the frissons, felt excluded. That's how a single stroke
of the pen on the marriage register distorted the frame
of our family for years. The crazy thing is, as kids,
thanks to his brilliant short cuts, the distant view of a spire

was the nearest we'd get to Sunday School. As my hands
struggled to hold his knee in line and guide his stiffened feet,
I'd sometimes remember how long before we fell to pieces
he once read me a poem on dying young and burying
his ashes at sea. The worst thing after he collapsed
to bear was seeing how the slightest thing made him cry.

Sometimes watching him slowly put together the pieces
of his fractured thoughts, trying not to lose his place
before he reached the end of his sentence, painfully leaning
his right arm on the table while his good hand strove to fall
again into the simplest tasks taken for granted till his stroke,
I'd wonder why for a time he'd changed so much, burying

family feeling and allowing us no room.
What really got to mum was him attending the Catholic
mass every Sunday and then he only goes and kids
her on for being a Proddy! Worse, he seemed to aspire
to being respectable, accusing her of crushing the frame
of his childhood, sending him away to school, though he found his feet

quickly enough, spending most of his time in one boat
or another. He was always brilliant with his hands.
While he was there he and the woodwork teacher built up
a whole fleet of them. Six years later when he finally collapsed
and died in hospital, I was too angry to cry.
At his funeral the kids and I played the Mozart Adagio and some jazz.

I couldn't cry. I kept thinking if he could see us he'd fall
about laughing like we always did since we were kids,
like the newspaper photo titled "Tranquility" mum kept in a frame
of him, his dog and his best mate in his favourite place
in a boat. I was so angry seeing my sister-in-law's collapsed
face as the doctor turned off the machine at a single stroke

and he died, shattering her belief in miracles to pieces.
It was then I understood it had always been her leaning
on him, not the other way round. She was all for burying
him with our lot – a bit late! – and I wasn't sure there'd be room.
How could I explain the poem and how, left in my hands,
I'd want it at sea? So he's by the sunlit trees in the Catholic

graveyard. Death in the family leaves you unsteady on your feet
for a long time. Three years later I did finally cry
buckets, having decided at last to torch the skeleton boat.
It was one hell of a heaven-singeing, uproarious pyre.
Seven years later his youngest took his clarinet up
and started stubbornly to teach herself to play jazz.

As You Die

For my brother, Bob

Into the valley of death
rode the five hundred
into the valley of death
hoofbeats thundering
heartbeats
into the valley
v   a   l   l   e   y
of death
you drifted
imperceptibly
heartbeats faltering
f   a   l   t   e   r   i   n   g
d   w   i   n   d   l   i   n   g
crossing the unknown frontier
fractured time
somewhere unseen
travelling into the indistinct beyond
beyond our knowing
t   r   a   v   e   l   l   i   n   g
to where we know you not.

Is it silent there?
Is the valley pale with asphodel?
Are the horsemen thundering through?
Do you feel us still
ghosts
r   e   c   e   d   i   n   g
into mists of tears?
Does the touch
of our warm hands
s   t   r   u   g   g   l   i   n   g
in vain
against the chill
restrain you
momentarily
as you pass through?
Accompanied
or alone?

Sole Survivor

Sole survivor
I came home
at last
to face
the household ghosts
arriving late reluctant and alone
in the dripping silence
of a wet midnight
soft with misty rain
expecting desolation
shadows of still raw grief
and found them
welcoming
- loving presences
solid as memory
physical as warmth
and vibrant with affection
waiting expectantly
in a house
empty and damp with winter
as spring broke through
the dark fettering soil
green and frantic
with resurrection
pushing grasses through the floorboards
and fox cubs scampering
beneath the beds at dead of night
in this slow silent occupation
verdant persistent
as growth
triumphant vernal upsurge.

Totem

On the horizon
I saw a fox
wild and brazen red
blade-running
down the tension line
sharp gleaming edge
where earth met sky
and sea encircled both
running lean and straight
auburn-gilded
as the sun
fell seaward
mist-diminished
into that opal moment
when day and night
hang poised
as the dusk hovers
breathless
in suspense.

Beach-combing

Walking along
the extreme edge of the shore
where the cliff's ribs fall
wind-stripped sun-blanched
into the sea
I spied an ammonite
and picked it up
delighted
letting slip my key
unnoticed
abandoned
along with my wedding ring
and various paraphernalia
of countless half-forgotten holidays
discarded
accidentally
over the years
haphazard offerings
to the corrosive gape
of the waves
sea change
of ritual omens.

Arriving home
I found
unfortunately
the fossil didn't fit
the keyhole
but came in handy
for breaking the window.

Accidental Application for a Poetic Licence

for Mario Rinvolucri

In my haste
to catch the post
and under strain
struggling to hold in balance
the rampant demands
of an imagination
which will no longer take
manana
for an answer
and the pressure
of life's machine-gun surface
I put the poems
carefully typed out for you
into the envelope
for the Inland Revenue.
I fully expected to receive
a dawn visit or a court summons
from the Ministry for Public Morality
but instead a letter arrived
on Her Majesty's Service
with a poetic licence
a dispensation for life
from paying income tax

even in the event
of my ever earning
enough to get over
the magic threshold
even if I became
utterly stinking
filthy rich -
fat chance!
At last
after years of receiving
tax returns full of zeros
under the weight of the poetic evidence
they've given up.

Generation

For my children, Joy and Spencer

These days
I face
the flash of steel
across the breakfast table
with slightly more composure
soundless scream
of tearing flesh
as generation
rends
from generation
in this age-old returning
casual brutality
of youth
as they leave home,
remembering
with what guilty alacrity
I turned a blind deliberate eye
against the depth-charged undertow
potent with fraught intuitions
and bereft beseechings of love
clawing voiceless at my green youth
and the bright briskness of my step
excitement-spurred
as I too once left home.

Childhood

For Joy and Spencer

The passing of the threshold
of their eighteenth birthday
beneath the joy and celebration
felt like a kind of dying
- body wound
which I took in my flesh
in that rotating supercission
of the old and fading
by the savage surgery of youth
as they spring up
triumphant
antler-crowned
from that primaeval killing field
of blood-strewn seed -
and I foresaw the ending
of my years of happiness
this little space of time
in which I struggled mind and hands
to forge some small stability
grappled ramshackle
out of the terror-stricken void

- safe haven
in the shifting sands of life
to shelter
their up-growing
and my own
as the house unfolded opening up rooms
desolate with dust-musty moss-damp emptiness
to hold their blossoming
the dank air rent with sunshine shouts
and quivering with startled shock
at the onrush of sudden games
clouding with dust from dancing feet
as music poured from the windows
flowing round the square of gardens
and I basked in the reflected glory
of those endless summer days of childhood
when time idles everlasting
suspended motionless
balanced on the upward-surging crest
before the wave peaks breaks and rushes on
in death-bound impetus
and my cascading hours slowed spellbound
tranced by the golden timelessness
of their ripening childhood years.

In Memoriam

For John Ireland, a brilliant and much loved teacher and life-long friend,
who taught me Latin and Greek, nourished my love of literature and the
structure of language, and showed me how to think and ask questions.

'quidquid amavimus, quidquid mirati sumus
manet mansurumque est'

Because you died
by your own hand
violently
in agony of mind
- you who in life
seemed so rational and gentle
given to reflection and discussion
rather than naked force of abrupt death
though it's true you could at times be cutting
rapier sharp
but who could guess what depth charge lay becalmed
as the imploding fuse of anger burnt
relentless through despair's corrosive crust
that catalysed
metaphor could suffer
such brutal metamorphosis
into the actual blade of sudden steel
turned cruel against yourself? -

because you died
we who survive remain haunted
by the ghosts of restless questions
which all too late
try to glimmer through the silence
grasp what lay behind your laughter
submit those impassioned conversations
-the wry throw-away phrases, caustic wit,
the way you looked, each familiar gesture –
to exhaustively rigorous
minute cross-examination
interrogations of memory
postmortems of emotion
vain soundings of the depths of complex pain
the unsuspected enigmatic force
which held you distant
so far close-guarded
beyond the loving impotence of friends.

Madun – Maiden Castle

Acre on acre of layered clouds
submit to limitation only
where the great trenches heaven-ward heave
in shimmering waves of wind-swept grass
as the pale sun rises transparent
lifted on lark song
through the overwhelming dark
of storm clouds
riven to the east
by gold-misted shafts fanned through
indigo
mirrored to the west
the tentative gleam of dawn
soft flushes
opal billowing vapour oceans
as timelessness holds the air entranced
at this hushed hallowed hour of vigil.

Nights on the Road

Recently it seems
I am subtly seduced
by the song of the road
under the whirring wheels'
exhilaration
speeding through black holes
of the headlamps' focus
where narrow hedgerow worlds
collapse light-sucked inwards
and car-encompassed
solitude pervades
the tunnel vacuum
down taut light corridors
through excluding darkness
obfuscating with
obscure shadow crowds
of ghostly travellers
foot soldiers toiling through
time-warped haunted furlongs
that I glide over
with such silken ease
slipping at dead of night
through bewitched dimensions
into the early hours
on the old straight road.

For Shoji Saikawa

My student and friend from Japan
who spent several summers with us.

Blue smoke curls hazy
in the morning sunlight, poised
like hesitant thoughts.

September Song

For Shoji

Sad September songs
sigh minor-modulating
- music of parting -

as autumn's fire flowers
red-flaring into winter
fall frost-defeated

geese-enchevronned skies
throb with the blood pulse of wings
and you fly eastward.

Thanks for the Encoded Messages

For Mario Rinvolucri and endless thanks for 60 years of
friendship, provocation and exchange of insightful insults.

Is this merely
just a piece of
information?

Is it a more than
usually subtle
exhortation
to gag my big gob?

Is it a veiled insult
a vile underhand
insinuation
concerning
my musicianship

imputation
that my superb
intonation
is less than perfect

recommendation
to mute myself
electronically?

Is it a belated
discreetly secretive
manifestation
of your possible
irritation
at my usually raucous
disapprobation
of the bloody Japanese?

Is it my paranoid
imagination?

Is it an astounded
exclamation
at the latest insanities
of modern existence

a surrealist
contemplation
on the violent
dislocation
caused by rapid
urbanisation

a subliminal
dissertation
on the recent
polarisation
of the Japanese psyche
and its enforced
refutation
of the intermediate zone

or an intellectual
observation
on Tokyo's spacial
deprivation?

Anyway
it made me shriek
sent me into
a wildly hysterical
ululation
of laughter.

So in final
peroration
and in deep appreciation

thanks for the encoded messages.

All Quiet on the Music Front

*'Thanks for the encoded messages' was my response to receiving
this article from Mario which at the time I found hilariously ludicrous.*

Anyone who lives next door to a budding musician can take heart from
an ensemble of devices from Yamaha, the Japanese musical instrument
manufacturer, which allow brass players, pianists and guitarists to practise
together without annoying everyone else within earshot.

For brass instruments, Yamaha has a £200 electric mute. When stuffed
into the bell of a trumpet or trombone it silences the instrument. But a
microphone inside the mute picks up remnants of the vibrations and feeds
them to a belt-mounted amplifier and headphones, allowing the musicians
to hear what they are playing.

The silent brass system can be used with Yamaha's £4000 silent piano, which
can also be made to produce sound only through the headphones. Pressing
a special pedal stops the hammers hitting the strings. Instead, light sensors
detect the speed at which the hammers move, and generate trigger signals.
These control a synthesiser which has been programmed to mimic the
sound of a piano.

Umbrella Talk

*In loving memory of the Dutch artist, Cees Landsaat, my dear friend and
constant inspiration for almost forty years from the day we met at art college
in London in 1971 until his death at the end of 2007 and of many
happy times we spent together in Amsterdam, Haarlem and England.*

Do you remember that day of gales
ripping amok through leaden clouds
whisking white spray across the polished steel
of puddled streets beribboned with canals
where we did battle ambushed at corners
by buffetings of hurtling gusts and squalls

and he strode on regardless, quite unmoved,
as you vainly flapped blue wings in protest
round his ears, did somersaults unnoticed,
turned inside out in tendon-tearing acrobatic feats
for nothing, while she, mindful of my safety,
furled in my elegant purple folds
at the first sign of danger
- "so considerate" – or so I thought?

Do you remember –
out of the storm
beyond the café threshold
lanterned and sophisticated
on that evening of luxurious relaxation –
how resplendently we reposed
side by side in an oriental vase
brilliant with peacocks and carnations
while they sat alone and talked and talked
and gazed into each other's eyes
as if the dusk would never end -
the world contained within that empty Chinese room
layered with the geometric sculpture
of precise pink table cloths

down a vista of chrysanthemums
mirrored as darkness falls beyond the window
in gleaming depths of water black as mystery
beneath the layered greens and reds
of formal foliage lashed
by the wildness of autumnal rain.
"This is the life" – or so I thought?

But then she went and left me
forgotten and abandoned in a foreign land
exposed to the dangerous playfulness of children
with their small heedless hands clutching at their prey,
left to weather the full force
of the most atrocious storms
and his neglectful nonchalance.
Oh for the peaceful and sophisticated café! -
where he never goes now she has gone,
just awaiting her return.

Birth Song for Seth

and in loving memory of my son-in-law, Neil,
who died 8 months before the birth of his son.

September – seeded,
summer – born, you slid shrouded
in dark blood, pulsed by

primal energies,
thrust out through throbbing caverns
irresistibly.

You emerged headlong
into the rent, silent shock
of explosive light.

Time stopped – awaiting
your first instinctive scream howled
from expanding lungs.

Birth's effort ended,
safe – entwined in loving arms,
life's small miracle,
fast asleep you lay.

Seth, because of you
round reft shadowlands of loss
we raise light structures
of potential joy.

Tenth Birthday Song for Seth

Lightning rips the far horizon.

The orange flash zips by again
over hill and down dale,
through sun, wind and rain
daring cloud, snow and hail.

Down muddy tracks he flashes by.
Where the hills greenly roll
he rides high,
always in control.

Down the woodland track he hurtles
laughing with reckless glee,
screeches round ninety-degree
bends defying gravity,
accelerating till he hits the jump
and soars in an arc through the air
landing, skidding sidewards
legs flexed, speed-elated
abruptly halts
breathless and exhilarated.

The Highway Code

It's cool
to go to school
and learn the Highway Code
and how to use it on the road,
so that other drivers know
where you intend to go
well before you do your moves.

Fifth Birthday Song for Rowan

Is it an angel?
Is it a kite?
No, it's Super – Spiderman
in flight.

Over bare hill-side, over wooded valley
through snow and tempest
across fields and lakes
westward powers Spiderman
to that distant land, always west
over the mountains rocky crest,
to wild Pentre faraway
where mighty Rowan,
Lord of the dragons,
whose wise rule all obey,
invites his superhero guests
to celebrate his fifth birthday.

"All hail, great lord!
We wish you Happy Birthday Five.
Accept this rare, gold dragonlet
to join your fiery flock.
May your dragons multiply and thrive.
May you long prosper and hold sway."
"Hail, Lord of the infinite Skies!
Your dragonlet is a most noble prize.
Our fiery thanks and welcome to our festive day."

And through the stormy waves flung spray
swims Superfrogman on his way.
" I am Superfrogman,
Guardian of the unfathomable Depths.
We wish you Many Happy Returns.
Lord Rowan is fishy-five today.
May you long prosper and hold sway.
Accept this giant birthday haddock
for your special delectation."
"Hail, Lord of the deepest Seas!
Our thanks and deep appreciation.
Welcome to our celebration."

Ninth Birthday Song for Rowan

If you go down to the lake today
you're in for a big surprise.
If you go down to the lake today
you'd better go in disguise -
for all the fishes from far and wide
shark, perch, pike, fish every size,
across the oceans, across the bay,
down countless rivers, from every side
have swum like mad to the lake today -
grunters and crappies, dace, roach and ray -
to see Rowan cast curving from the skies,
his rainbow of multi-coloured flies.

A Glamorous Day Out with Miss Léonie

Whenever I possibly can
I go to have my hair done
at the unequalled, the one and only
Hair Salón Miss Léonie.
She can make you over
like you've never been before.

Even though it's lockdown time
cramped in by Covid 19,
Miss Léonie is still queen
of glamour and chic French style
with her je ne sais quoi sublime.

Her colour combination
is a rainbow sensation -
eyelids shaded with aquamarine
highlighted with a delicate mist
of glitter tinted with amethyst.

Then we whisk home for a quick change
into something sleek and glamorous
colour-themed with our eye blush.
Then off to Sushi Nara
for our favourite light supper
before dancing the night away
at Night Club Sayonara
where Miss Léonie demonstrates
the latest steps and thrilling routines
and she puts me through my paces
in contemporary and jazz
with zest and creative pzazz.

Miss Léonie's prices reflect
her high skills and quality
but luckily for me
after this luxuriously extravagant day
I don't even have to pay.
Miss Léonie is my grand daughter,
aged nine, so I receive
a generous "granma" discount
for make believe.

THE YEAR OF JAPAN

INTRODUCTION

In 1985 I started working as a freelance teacher of English as a foreign language and much of my work was for a local Japanese Company who employed me to teach some of their staff and their families. I taught the men at my home after they finished work and their wives at their homes during the day. All lessons were one-to-one. I worked for the Company in this way for over twenty years, taking on new employees as they arrived here.

Seiya Kobayashi, the subject of "The Year of Japan" arrived at my house one day in July 1992, unannounced and accompanied by a senior manager. Seiya was about thirty at the time and was an accountant working as Accounts Co-ordinator, which meant he co-ordinated the accounts between the parent company in Japan and the branch companies in England, Germany and America. Because of the time differences he often had to work late at night and generally seemed to work long hours and be under a lot of pressure, so he was often late and sometimes couldn't make it at all. Unlike his colleagues, he hadn't wanted to come abroad and didn't like being in England – in fact, he seemed very unhappy when I first met him. He was unmarried and lived alone. He was also the shyest person I've ever met and for a long time he was almost completely tongue-tied, so teaching him required considerable efforts of ingenuity and application to get him going at all. Even his work colleagues said he was an extremely shy and quiet man. From July 1992 until February 1993 (the date when "The Year of Japan" begins) I taught him one hour a week. In February I suddenly had the idea that switching over roles somewhat might make it easier for him to talk, so I suggested very tentatively that perhaps he might like to come for a second free hour when he would teach me some Japanese words and answer my questions about Japan and for the other hour, which the company paid for, we could continue English lessons as usual. To my great amazement he accepted this idea and actually seemed very pleased. So, we adopted this plan for the rest of that year and until April 1994 when he went back to Japan.

Working with a student who has such extreme difficulties with communication and the effort required to get some insight into their emotional world is the work of the imagination and I personally can't do it without a high degree of emotional involvement. Sometimes therefore it feels like a kind of love affair. At the same time it's crucial to differentiate rigorously between fantasy and reality and to hold the tension at all times. So, the poems are written and read as a series of love poems, but they describe my interior world as opposed to my teaching practice, which was always completely professional. I was just over fifty at that time, so I had a lot of experience in disciplining and holding this kind of emotional tension and I was aware of the comic aspects of the situation. Because I could feel how unhappy he was during the early months of our acquaintance from July 1992 and through the first winter and because I could see how isolated he was and how much pressure he was under at work, I did everything I could to make the time that he spent with me enjoyable and relaxing and I was constantly trying to invent teaching strategies to make it easier for him to express himself. It's quite usual for Japanese men to be inhibited by their fear of losing face if they make a mistake. However, in Seiya's case I always felt his diffidence and self-containment were much deeper than superficial reactions to outward stimuli and were much more essential characteristics of his interior emotional landscape. He once told me his first name meant "the sighing of the wind" and his surname "the small dark forest", both of which seemed deeply appropriate.

Tags...

For Seiya

Silence sighing in the trees
softly as the wind
lightly shimmers
through dappling shadows –
still music in the forest's darkness.

So your laughter
glancing off the surface shyness
ripples singing
through the quiet depths
of your calm stillness' deep dark waters.

My Eyes into Japan

This year
winter ended
on the February evening
we made our diffident bargain,
and you agreed
to my surprise
to become
my eyes into Japan,
offering me glimpses of light
into the opaque mystery world
that lies behind
the closed frontiers of your eyes
in exchange
for business English
and unspoken passion.

I Throw Open the Window

I throw open the window
and there you are
running down the garden path
suddenly informal
almost childlike.

Momentarily watching
your slim small form
- the dark hair
and oriental face,
immaculate clothes
and briefcase
clutched beneath your arm -
running incongruously
down an English garden path
in March,
I remember
how you walked briskly
business-like
into my life
one July afternoon,
all stiff formality
and shy confusion,
your face slammed shut
against my Englishness,
as I lay swinging
in a sunlit hammock,
wrenched from my books,
stunned, unbelieving,
as you walked past me,
dreamlike and surreal

and my rapt heart
turns over.

All That Time Allows

I lie awake,
the shroud of sleep
ripped suddenly away,
stark naked,
not a shred of drowsiness
or dream
to shelter me.
Four o'clock
on a morning crisp with stars.

Desire strikes
like fever seeping through the blood
as images of your body torture me,
intense and palpable,
dark hair and muscularity
smooth beneath my hands,
your small compactness
taut within my arms,
resistance loosening
as my lips ravish yours
with greedy tenderness,
delirious with your beauty.

Breathless fantasies
chasing through my mind
in full flight reined back hard,
as I remember
my faltering body,
no longer young,
slackening –
slow corruption creeping unseen
through the flesh,
the spirit yearning
though the flesh is weak,
not even weak – unlovely
to another's youth-blind eyes:
and I reel back
from your alluring image
- youthful beauty,
untouched,

unattainable -
into the dark abyss,
racked between passion and mortality,
bound without mercy
on the wheel
that turns relentless,
poised within
the twin-poled tension
- sex and death.

Is this impassioned torture
all that time allows,
as shadows start to gather
at the darkening margins
of my sunlit days
and silence lurks,
deep as the grave,
somewhere just beyond
the dying fall of music
and the lull of voices,
as I confront
the fragile loveliness
of yet another transient spring
and feel,
within the summer's scent-hazed heat,
the hovering chill
dark-winging
through my time-fused fleeting hours
and death-skimmed dreams of passion?

That Autumn of Bereavement

It was endless dark descending
that long autumn of bereavement
when you and I staggered shell-shocked
stranded deep in grief's grey wasteland,
iced-up, cut-off,
through reeling days,
becalmed, befogged
upon a winter sea of pain,
passed parallel through hells of loss
and chanced to meet,
feeling faint tremors through the chill
benumbing dark opacity
- slow autumn sluggish with despair
which solaced by your sadness found
a transmutation – out of loss
brings an unexpected freedom.

Hanten*

It was a Sunday morning
liquid with daffodils and scudding showers
when I arrived
armed with my alibi,
unannounced,
and took you by surprise
as you opened the door,
your face pale and shuttered,
limpid dark eyes distant
with recent drowsiness
and cherry-blossom dreams
drifting
beneath snow-capped mountains,
pale glittering volcanoes,
festive,
dazzling,
in your Sunday clothes
the turquoise blaze
bright across your chest,
dark shirt,
perfect white trousers
- azure sea,
pine-shadow blackness,
distant snows
reflecting
in your eyes
- cool distance
melting
as we talk
translucent
into warmth.

Sunday best

The Soft Sigh of Farewell Is Built into Your Name

All
aware
suddenly
knowing full well
as I'd always done
from that giddy moment
when my wakened heart spun round
three hundred and sixty degrees
in a split fraction of a second
that there could
only
be
no hope
no future
no ongoing
continuity
no cooling-off process,
that the soft sigh of farewell
is built into your name
inevitably
sayonara
willingly,
Seiya,
or
no,
laughing
ruefully
in the face of
life's absurdity,
resolutely reckless
to the end – I decided
true to myself to let feeling
soar, joyous passionate free-flying
till
farewell
brings silence
and an
end.

Iki Masho I*

Can't you
just once
or twice
break out
of your shyness,
knock your schedule
sidewards,
let go
of the curtain
of your caution,
shielding
you from
these imagined,
self-inflicted
dangers
lurking
in the dark streets
of the city
- curtains
are so
insubstantial
just swish through them.
Pluck up
courage
- Japanese is
rich in rudeness,
using
grammar
to be cutting
- structured insults!
English
just has
crude expletives!

Make your choice in
either
language
then
abruptly tell
your bloody boss
to go to hell,
get stuffed,
or some
short Japanese
equivalent.
And
at least
just for
one long evening
let your hair down,
and come
with me
and hit the town,
let pleasure rip
and drink
and dance
till the music
ceases softly,
dying
cadence
falling
gently,
darkness
fading,
homeward
speeding
with the dawn.

Let's go

Iki Masho II

I could just kidnap you
- pleasure's passionate guerrilla
in a rainbow balaclava
militant for long holidays
and free time
against the grey wastes
of Capitalism
with a capital English 'C'
or a Japanese 'shi'
- and rescue you from your schedule
- it's easier for me – schedules
are so foreign to my nature -
and carry you off
protesting
for three months holiday
or more maybe, depending on
when they paid the ransom
and the exchange rate mechanism
- a gentleman's sworn agreement,
nothing in writing – or hard cash
already spent well in advance
on our UK tour – then
Paris, Copenhagen, Madrid,
Vienna, Amsterdam,
anywhere you want to sightsee
- your Japanese efficiency
tempered with my random approach.
Then at last,
if you really yearned
for work and company,
I'd hand you over gracefully
- till next summer maybe?

Sakura[*]

Cherry blossom
in Japanese
is spelt like
Greek for sweetness,
pronounced like
sacra,
sacred things in Latin.
This year
because of you
I counted it
among those things
which I hold sacred
and left it
as an offering
on your doorstep
- affectionate
propitiation,
memory -
in this obscure sunset outpost
where you stand
- conscript of the eastern empire
winged from half way round the world,
unlikely Hermes -
as guardian of the threshold
of my dark rites of passage
through secret seasons
of the flesh
and spirit,
last accounts' coordinator
of the unfinished business
for my years' ending.

Cherry blossom

Maybe

Meanwhile
the cherry blossom frothed to fullness
overflowed
and fell
- I swear
you'd not have noticed
had I not left some
on your doorstep-
the garden
flower-flooded
overnight
and summer blazed
regal in lilac
resplendent in peonies
on my birthday,
which this year you share,
the usual pallor of your face
just slightly flushed with wine
below your eyes,
as we eat
and wander
in each other's wordland
down the sinuous desire paths of language
exploring obscure glades of dappled shadows
where meaning shimmers intertwined with feeling's
flowing rainbow of chameleon colours,
and you tell me
how the clear-cut harsh definity of English
beside the liquid suppleness of Japanese
makes promising
feel difficult
- imposed constriction
on the future's
unknowable uncertainty
with no escape clause.

And I watch the flow
of feeling
flickering
across your face,
etching on memory
mood-light and shadow
of your passing thoughts
in these snatched hours
which I await
with such intensity of pleasure
and something recently like calm,
as I attune myself more finely,
senses vibrating in sympathy,
melody freely modulating
with the fluctuations of your life.

And when you go
you leave behind
your promise,
fluid as maybe,
as a gift.

The Consolidated Accounts

The consolidated accounts,
you say,
will be finished
next week
and you'll be free
- maybe......

I wish, by all the gods,
that my accounts would
consolidate
instead of slipping
through the nerveless fingers
of my memory
like globules of quicksilver
from a broken flask,
propelled haywire
in all directions
by the imperious pressures
of much more important business -
imagination's
throbbing blood pulse
through my heart and brain.

Deep Time I

The rainbow drops of time I spend with you
are glistening prisms fracturing the shaft
of concentrated light and energy
into myriad opaline liquid
images,
multi-faceted, jewel-bright mirrors
filtering
the white-hot crazing current of soul-light,
danger-charged
until it earths and finds its outlet through
this burning brilliant held intensity
of our ephemeral dwindling time space.

Deep Time II

These few hours of deep-sea time
I spend with you
send subterranean forces
tidal-waving
through the time-loaded layers
of my geology,
exploding with volcano energy
memory's mirror to experience,
bursting through fault lines of my reluctant
barricaded consciousness,
dredging up from the bedrock
of inheritance
haphazard depth-scoured flotsam,
storm-tossed sea drift
of small hard-core knowledges
worn down, hard won
from raw-edged jags of pain
by the patient passage of the years
- fragments
which current-swept together
reassemble,
coalesce tidal-sculpted,
water-beaten
into reconstructed forms,
as calm descends,
dawn-lustrous,
on the fresh-hewn shore
of my mythology.

Bank Holiday

This time
when I took you by surprise,
calling late in the evening
at an hour when even you
would have left work and come home,
your face was open and your smile
held pleasure and that half amused,
lip-tilting, eye-glinting, much-loved
expectant curiosity
which recently lights up our talk;
and you let me
step over the guarded frontier
of your doorway,
trespass
on forbidden territory
one single step
out of the evening's mild damp dusk
into the light
where you stand out of uniform,
barefoot

- the sudden erotic
vulnerability
of your small brown perfectly-formed
bare feet
brought close,
as, stooping, I retrieve my pen
and reel
with desire to touch, caressing
their small-boned delicate sculpted
beauty,
but I straighten and concentrate
my mind
on the map we hold together,
explaining possibilities
of geography for your journey,
as my senses bathe in the full
festive
summer closeness of your body,
exchanging the kind of smiles that,
centre-seeking,
dart through the eyes and pierce the soul,
before I step outside and say
goodnight.

Remembering the Fall of Saigon, April 30th 1975

When the empire leaves
I shall suffer the fate
of those who are won over
by the strange and foreign
and, magicked
by the lure
of language,
trust that
understanding
with the enemy
is possible
- brokers
who mediate
for love or profit
between cultures
- adventurers
who thrill to the siren sweet
ambiguous shadowlands
and lose their hearts
on the wrong side
of the frontier

- messengers across the lines
- interpreters
- all those who
venture their vulnerability
balancing on cobweb bridges
carved from mother of pearl,
complex and delicate
as filigree,
thrown tightrope frail
across the treacherous quicksands
of no-man's-land,
and pit the heart's fragility
against the barriers of custom
- all those who
at the last
abandoned
washed up
shallows-stranded
amidst the wreckage
of their fortunes,
stricken,
watch the last boat
cast anchor slowly
sliding seaward,
as the empire leaves
for ever.

Musing

In fact
you're useless
as a muse –
muses are supposed
to loll around relaxedly
with their clothes in erotic disarray
waiting on the artist's pleasure,
but you
are always
dashing back
straight to the office
mega-stressed and immaculate
in your well-pressed grey suit – not a moment
to spare as the faxes pile up,
immune,
politely resistant
to all my attempts
to slow down time's hurtling passage
and get you to dally artistically
and prolong these few precious hours
- well once,
this summer's
one hot day
you did actually
consent to sit on the hammock
sideways with your feet firmly on the ground,
but flatly refused to lie back
feet up
and relax
languidly
even when you got
slightly tipsy and flushed with wine,
though you did begin to swing to and fro
gently before leaving for work.

Worse still,
you are a man
- a singularly manly man.
Who's heard of a masculine muse,
when poetesses are supposed
to get by somehow on their own
inspiration,
be Sapphicly self-sufficient
or even hermaphroditic
and unbemused?

And even worse,
you are from a culture
where men expect to be
haughtily dominant
and take the active part,
always hidden behind
the all-embracing mask
of uniformity,
shaped to conform and shun
the individual,
trained to repress the self
in favour of the mass,
where the delights of fantasy
are officially scheduled out
- imagination's forbidden flowering
struggles etiolating in the dark.

Maybe
in this age
of commerce,
lines-written-per-hour-
poets-in-residential-homes-
keep-potential-subversives-inside-out-
of-community-care-fully-
gagged-bound-
paraded-
publicly-
in-chic-seminars-
inspiration-sold-with-coffee-
cash-in-on-interesting-minorities-
maximum productivity,
muses
can't survive -

are passée
with their pastoral
idylls of generosity
and profligate riches of timelessness,
made for infinite dalliance,
and – like
the great god
Pan – are dead,
departed elsewhere,
redundant divines in excess,
reluctant refugees left over from
an unhurried unmoneyed past.

And I
out of joint
out of date
should abandon you
- get modern and profitable,
shrewd, disciplined and market-researchful,
untantalised by temptation,
but I
remember
how you once
twisted hands in hair
as language failed across the gulf,
torn between wanting and required duty,
physical and fraught with longing,
and I
can't leave you,
frustrating
complex mystery,
who send my thoughts scintillating
in wild cascades across uncharted stars
or leave me stranded high and dry,
wordless
dumbfounded
blankly mute
alone and stifled
in my private silent wasteland,
or pierce with tidal shafts of clarity
as the lens' brilliance shutters down,
deep sea
unfathomed
as you are.

High Risk Magic on the Run

I arrived with quarter of an hour to spare
after driving halfway across the country,
while you got there on the dot slightly breathless,
announcing you had to leave an hour early
to rush back to work for the rest of tonight,
so this week we did manage both to be there
in the same place
at the same time
for one short heady hour,
vibrant with the excitement of holidays.
And you confessed
that last year during the holidays
you were sent off on a business trip
because you were new and unscheduled
- and too shell-shocked to dare to say no -
I suggested.
You didn't understand the word 'dare'
but were at home with 'high risk factor'.
So I showed you
- given the lack of time for teaching
more complex potent deep enchantments -
how to placate the gods of pleasure,
ensure good luck
and keep the demons of work at bay
this summer
by touching wood
and keeping your fingers tightly crossed,
and you searched hard
for similar gestures in Japan
for times like these,
and you found absolutely nothing
- not surprising!

The Year of Japan I

This is the year of Japan
this lucid year of clarity
when I see through the riddle,
read the maze's innermost secrets,
reinterpret codes,
arrive at answers
sought through all these years of dreaming,
and thus at last enlightened
have escaped the Sphinx's circling deaths
by self-destruction:

this wondrous year of sorcery
when I have found the alchemy,
the hidden stone of transformation
seen dimly through the fumes of striving,
catalyst of change
and revelation
glowing in the depths of darkness,
visible to those who venture
plummeting dark-night, deep-sea journeys,
hurtling through black holes of the spirit
beyond that unplumbed dread descent:

this complex year of paradox
when the equation's cloudy essence,
thus catalysed, turned lucid and shone clear
as innate inequality
- positive equals negative -
- inspiration is almost like love -
but not – this Delphic knot
of self-delusion, unloosed, resistant
to half a lifetime of unravelling,
fell suddenly apart,
and through the smoke-hazed cavern
gloomed with prophecies and dreams,
unblinded, undazzled,
at last I saw distinct
the taut-tensioned mystery

of held-apart polarity,
and ceased to pour that dark energy's
exploding abstract force
imploding through love's fragile circuits:

this limpid year of signs and messages
of recognition
when I received the messenger
and, moved by his beauty and his strangeness,
embraced the meaning, held his words,
without vain striving to impede his flight
or lure him earthward
- luminous inspiring angel,
bright meteor at risk of falling light-quenched
into night of my desiring;
when I perceived the power of totems
and read the visionary moments
of the red fox in sun-tinged arrow flight
blade-running down the quivering tension line,
and geese in steely nomad chevrons blazed
and throbbed across a copper solstice sky,
as darkening meadows glimmered
with the light of secret candles:

this austere year of self-restraint
stretched between worlds so disparate
when I have learnt to balance,
hold taut
the intricate discipline
of the dance's measured patterns
that hold my feet unfaltering
within the dervish ecstasy
of high exhilaration,
tight-tensed
between obsession's madness
and the search for meaning there
within
where I am most in danger,
running straight down the tension line,
intense and focused,
keeping all my worlds in orbit
separate-circling:

this Persephone year of contrast
which began
underworld
dungeoned-deep
imprisoned
powerless
held in thrall
by darkness
held helpless
deep in labyrinthine passages
where despair
leads me down
encircled
circling round
returning
tortuous
nightmare tracks
whose tortured
twisting through disorientation
found no way
out:
prisoner
by powers of darkness night-enravished
imprisoned
underworld
found within
helpless hands
a thin thread
tenuous
frail as love
which yet held
and drew me upwards shadow-ensnared
yet surface-soaring and unfettered
as light bursts
and earth-bound spring breaks green and potent
out of night:
the earth splits
rent apart between light and darkness
sundered pregnant into fruitfulness
goddess-freed
empowered
energised:

this harvest year of integration
when the elements
all combined
and coincided into ripening,
found their destined time
of harvest,
after circling seasons of sorrow
when pain's slow pulsing
drop by drop
fell upon the heart insistent as
sleepless memory,
till at last,
in despair, against my stubborn will,
comes understanding
full of grace,
that time's straight arrow curves concentric
into circles
where rites of passage lead
our endangered faltering footsteps
full of fear
across the angel-guarded thresholds
awe-inspired
traversing through revolving cycles
transcendent
merciful
redemptive.

The Year of Japan II

For Shoji Saikawa

This is the year of Japan,
the year when I transformed
my heart's becluttered vaults
encumbered with
extravagance of passion
importunate longings
hopeless expectations
lust's fraught fevers
- vanities

into a sparse interior
of calm serenity
and found within
this quiet simplicity
an unsought richness unrevealed
by all my frenzied searchings;

and on a morning misty
with unsuspecting dreams
received in confirmation
from the furthest limits
of your journey to the north
a dove bearing peace and flowers
- messenger.

Sayonara

I always knew
that someday parting
was inevitable

for I
am of the floating world

- that cobweb raft
of fantasy
whose shimmering landscapes
insubstantial
rise structured on
the driftwood of the mind
enmeshed within
a web of dreams –

and I
have bartered all my sure
infrastructured
safe certainties
for imagination's
shifting shadow play
of mirages

while you
belong
to the mainland
firmly anchored to
the material world
of confident solidity

and have
a well-mapped life
of constant schedules
and ranking hierarchies
structured in ambition

and all my work
of building bridges
failed to span the distance.

BENDING THE RULES

Introduction

By 1997 I was doing occasional short periods of teaching at a centre in Canterbury which specialised in business English for company executives and workers at a high level. They typically already spoke good English so their aspirations were ambitious and aimed at native – speaker level.

This was where I met Tomoo Shimizu, a Japanese man in his early thirties who was working for a large Japanese company as a technical salesman. He already had an excellent command of English and good accuracy and as head of Asian and European Sales he was already using English daily in his work for telephone calls on complex technical subjects. He was in England for a few weeks to further improve his English paid for by his company. I taught him for two weeks on the intensive one – to – one course which meant a four hour session 9am-1pm and another two hours 4pm-6pm daily. He had a group session with another teacher from 2-4pm.

He had already been at another school for a month and seemed disillusioned and discouraged with his progress. He was extremely tense and frequently very tired as if suffering from depression, and his extreme fear of making mistakes and trying out new language and methods was seriously inhibiting his self – expression.. To cut through these problems I changed the usual daily routines and tried to move out of the classroom which he seemed to associate with the strains and pressures of his workplace. He was a very intelligent and sensitive person with an unusually wide range of interests, including science and art ceramics. I found there were exhibitions of both these subjects in the town and got reluctant permission from the centre to spend some time there. As I expected, once in an environment embodying his passions, he forgot his fears and immediately relaxed into excited, self – expressive talk both to me and to exhibition staff, giving him practice with native speakers in a natural situation. We then used the materiel and vocabulary from outside back in the classroom. By changing my own usual teaching routines I tried to mirror the changes I was trying to bring about in him to help him confront his negative delusions about his abilities more realistically.

Bending the Rules

For Tomoo Shimizu

Was it delusion? Delirious dreaming?
No,
it definitely happened
daily
nine
ten
eleven
twelve
where I waited
each morning at nine in the upstairs room
heavy with the scent of spring
just breaking through the window
where storm clouds loom and zoom
exultant
and you came.
Punctuality's the rule there
until we bent it.

Do you remember,
Shimizu, spilling secrets
into my cupped hands?

Letting me step right
now out of the upstairs room
across the threshold

of Sapporo dreams
where girls glance across the streets
and company days

where revolution
is just a contained whisper
of mute discontent?

Of my blind fingers
catching reverberations
across strung spaces?

Perhaps

I should set up my
academy of passion
for fallers–in-love

- I am quite probably
the leading world authority
and what's more I'm living:
so many of the world's
great lovers don't survive -

presiding half-way
between an aging geisha
and a sorceress

and weave my spells of
loving entanglement for
mute Japanese men

quietly despairing
round about thirty something
as time narrows down

inexorably
in the crowded solitude
of faceless Tokyo

in the small rooms of
company dormitories
of impassioned love

slightly thinning hair
and unarranged marriage with
fantasy girlfriends

in no-woman's land
of those solitary free hours
ten
eleven
twelve

one am.

In the upstairs room,
Shimizu, silence too speaks
across strung spaces.

There we underwent
the pain of transmutation
- mute sadness of thoughts

which fail to survive
through the thronging migration
language to language

and fall fluttering
drowned in the depths of silence
mutely expiring.

And how intensely
how we strove to surface them
like mediums entranced

searching for voices
among the whispering ghosts
of our latency.

The upstairs room fills
with the resounding silence
of our presences

as we integrate
our effort of transmission
pulsing charge to charge

across strung spaces
daring the middle passage
of sub-surface loss.

Do thoughts transmit from
culture to culture intact
submerged and gliding

through interfaces
surviving the violence
of transmutation?

Can our mute pulses
incarnate themselves in sound?
Do thoughts transmit or

are we prisoners
forever of our culture
deep-sea islanded?

Do you remember
choirs of electronically
silenced saxophones,

Shimizu, softly
in evensong unison
hymning the fading

of the light as dusk
filters through sonorous depths
of arching echoes?

In the upstairs room
darkness sifts through our absence
gathering whispers

of our resonance
suspended and awaiting
the dawning of light.

The sudden mysteries
of latency dream of dawn
and embodiment.

Overnight brilliance
of spring fills the upstairs room
bathed in pale sunlight

where sea moon glows blue
hazed in alchemy of glass
and molten streams burn

red and metallic
flowing in lustrous swathes round
undulating forms.

There as you enter
I watch the shock reflected
in your dazzled eyes.

For you I became
subversive bending the rules
of life and language

and the upstairs room
blazes sensual with colours
of dreams and passions.

In that furnace fire
I bent the rigid metal
of our routined minds

melted rutted fears
loosed encumbering structures of
reinforced custom.

Do you remember,
Shimizu, clearing safety
barriers and props

- in those freed spaces
responding to fast fleeting
moments of impulse

dancing right now through
compelling complexities
unfettered by rules?

How sinuously
language flows round fugitive
forms and images

slipping supple curves
round shimmering nuances
of subtle meaning.

The upstairs room is
electric with energy
as we risk the charge

of catalysis
in exploding alchemies
of mind-changed magic

infringing frontiers
by the outward thrust of walls
expanding spaces.

As time closes down
pain cuts through the strung spaces
of the upstairs room

rending transmission,
and my invaded dreams face
the tearing anguish,

as vulnerable with
shared secrets, you close the door
on our openness.

There two weeks before
I walked into the ambush
unaware and pressed

the concentrated
essence of your unknown life
into that fraught phial

from whose tight span you
pour the released energy
of adolescence.

Transmission fades and
falters across strung spaces
shuddering with shock.

Silence no longer
vibrates across strung spaces
in the upstairs room

where we shall never
greet again the prisoner
and stranger enclosed

within weak walls nor
undergo that vibrant shock
of recognition.

Beyond the empty
spaces of the upstairs room
silence, Shimizu,

is still

also an answer.

MEETINGS WITH ANGELS ON THE DANCE FLOOR OF RANDOM CHANCE

In appreciative memory of the fantastic dance and music scene in 1990's Birmingham and especially of Moseley Dance Centre, the original "dance floor of random chance" with its wondrous African and Latin-American bands every Saturday night and the harmonious, friendly, multi-racial crowd of dancers who participated

The Dance Floor of Random Chance

For Fredrick Mwanza

At the end of the evening
on the dance floor of random chance
when you begged me
repeatedly
to take you home
I laughed cynically in your face
unbelieving and sarcastic
- later I understood
how drunk or desperate
you must have been
to be so shy
and so importunate
with a total stranger -
- or was it that already
we both recognised
each other's touchier than usual
risky fragility
and deep beneath the surface
felt at ease? -
but at the time
it wasn't at all apparent
and I thought what a bloody cheek you had
warned you about getting into cars with strangers
and going home with voracious older women
who might eat you up for breakfast
and your eyes widened momentarily
glinting whitely in the half-light
and then you grinned and said
you thought you could trust me.

Nevertheless
- after the ritual exchanges
written on torn halves
of the same scrap of paper
fragile talismans
entrusted so carelessly
with troubling intimations
precocious desires

potentialities
vibrations -
that night
I did go home alone.
But during the ensuing days
memories
of all the warm exuberance
and the force of feeling
- some childlike poignancy -
behind your plea
kept stopping me in my tracks
refusing to be dismissed.
So when we met again
by accident
on the dance floor of random chance
and the hearts on our sleeves
hesitant and eager
in those split infinite instants
which palpitate between
the rapture of recognition
and acceptance
trembled wildly
in anticipation
I eventually gave in
and took you home.

Of course
away
from the dance floor of random chance
life proved more complex
and sometimes pain
slipped its talonned fingers
into the interstices
of our easy passion
and sometimes fear
infiltrated
affectionate intimacies
deviating
tenderness
complicating
innocence.
Imagined betrayals
misunderstandings
sometimes happened.

Nevertheless
that moment of meeting
when life in its wondrous waywardness
crossed our steps
on the dance floor of random chance
and you asked me to dance
and took my hands
to guide me into the intricacies
of your rhythm
still seems to me
some parcel-from-paradise
star-blest miracle.

For Fredrick

My black and searing angel
fallen
physical
real
corporeal
amidst the sweat and hustle
of the dance floor
whose loose undulating suppleness
flows dark and liquidly
along the subtleties of rhythm
as drum beats throb incarnate
pulsing pelvic chants of Africa
made flesh within your loins,
and your black radiance
burns, drinking in the darkness,
smoulders light-reflecting
as strobe lights twist and shimmer
glowing smooth and silken
in the dark pool of your skin,

whose lithe and lovely
lazy sensuality
lasers through my last
lingering vacillations,
reluctant vanquished
memories
of cool lustless calm
clinging to intimations
of serenity,
cynical protestations,
frayed ends of sexless
nirvana.

And so I plunge
defenceless
free-falling
floating
sinking
through translucent depths
of that sensual ocean
in which desire holds me close
as death, expiring on a sigh,
submerged, disintegrating
as gender merges
and our fused limbs flow molten
round the dark core of your heat
then fall extinguished,
as breathless you exhale me
and your light body loosens
lax and melting into darkness
drifts down along the dream paths
softly into sleep.

Leaving Eden

For Fredrick

At first
it was only Eden
and innocence
and fresh green-appled dawn
generous, luxuriant, delicious
with unforbidden fruits,
a merging closeness of melting touch,
an unconditional surrender
sensual selfless sliding into bliss
which knew no barriers
like slipping through the net
of this muddled muddied
guilt-entrammelled flawed mortality
clean into a clarity of stars.

But fear crept in
slithering and devious
suddenly insinuating treachery
and you recoiled
as age-old memories stirred
drumming dark and visceral within the blood
of rigorous rites of manhood
where slender adolescents passed
into the harsh and murderous
society of men
in utter exile from
the dangerous diversionary desirability
the soft seductive sweetness
of the women's house
into which I unknowingly abducted you,
a willing longing ambivalent accomplice
in our passionate collusions
of transgression.

And you retreated
and excluded me.
And I bereft and lonely
battered myself against

the iron-muscled walls
beat on the armour-plated shell
the uncomprehending enclosed
world of men
to find you
fluttering vainly broken-winged
until I fell to ground
where I who always found
the soaring ecstasy of fantasy
more real than harsh reality
who raging savage at the hurt
of the body's broken promises all
unfulfilled
wrought havoc
smashed whatever else remained,
for love of you
made treaties with my anger
tore them up
rewrote my calm,
for love of you
began to search for other ways
recovering courage and transcending pain
- embarked upon researches
down through darkening corridors
to penetrate the depth-dusky recesses,
raided stuffed storehouses stealthy with secrets
looted barricaded larders loaded full
with undisturbed decades of hoarded riches,
and retrieved
memories
of sultry troubled adolescent summers
heavy with desire and guilty with
shimmering auras of tabooed temptations
of the confused deliciousness of
caressing fingers softly stroking
the awe-tensed and terror-stricken skin
under half-intuited shadows
of unspeakable evil-omened
immanencies
- evolved compassionate interpretations
dredged up long perspectives
on the tidal ebb and flow
of your anxieties
and drew up resilient adumbrations
of informed tenderness
out of the world's complexity.

While you made efforts
risking yourself in
flights of courage and intelligence
beyond my guessing
into unfamiliar alien worlds
moving hesitant
and careful between opposing camps
crossing the dance floor
at moments of enthusiasm
to dance with your friends
the tight-encircling celebratory
dance of manhood
yet always coming back
to me in reconciliation.

And together
we have built bridges
against the odds
painstaking engineerings of trust
girdering across rent distances
of space and time and race
light temporary structures
of unsuspected strength
versatile and adaptable
for sudden surprise sallies
and changing circumstances
in an insecure world.
And latterly
we have taken up arms
against the old enemy
venturing hand in hand
on affectionate crusades
against anxiety.

And love
outside of Eden
does still hold.

For Fredrick

The night before you left
to settle your nerves
and put off the hour of parting
I did a small-hours raid
on the wreckage of my room
ransacking the chaos
in a wild search for gifts
precious but small enough
to fit into your pockets
for some of the members
of your very extended family
giggling inwardly at
ironic echoes of
condescending colonial stories
of baubles for the natives
and trying hard to forget
as I came up with dozens
of assorted pairs of ear-rings
and multi-coloured teddy bears
that this year is merely a rehearsal

while you lounged on the bed
slender and feline
and reclined swigging back the wine
with the soles of your upturned feet
glowing softly pink
and your kisses burned
seared across memory
and your laughter gleamed
like mother-of-pearl
set in ebony
in the hazy dusk
beyond the lamp light's halo.

Songs of Love and Darkness and Disappeared Histories

For Fredrick

The black silk velvet
of your skin
melts into darkness
marginless
all outline swallowed seamless
by surrounding shadows

merges with Mau Mau memories
mute with night-encroaching ghosts
gliding
murderous and menacing
into the lethal darkness
bent on
violence on violence
avenging past-laden horrors
heaped high
accrued through white centuries of
cruelty on cruelty

envelopes me
engulfed and mellow
as I bask
within the glowing gorgeous glossiness
black-burnished
of your lamp-lit limbs
beneath my touch

submerges me
yielding as I plunge
surrendered
to the secret shame-shy depths of blackness
where the budding rose swells flushed and rises
caress-empowered bursts blushing into flower
refulgent in the flames of our desire
throbs and falls
quiescent darkening
night-enfolded

lies held within
the white encircling
of my arms
close-enlaced against the melting margins
where darkness seeps into your slender curve
dissolves the supple contours of your form
and seeks to steal your sleep-tranced beauty
from my sight
across the threshold
of oblivion
where I stand guard
and as you turn
momentary words
materialise
in the gleam
caught lip-read from the whiteness of your teeth
of faint whisperings from the slumber verge
as you float disembodied into sleep
and my watching eyes traduced endrowsied
sleep-suborned
follow you miraged
in mists of dreams

stands in contrast
beside the paleness
of my skin
where the slender columns of our arms lie
smooth-polished ebony to rough-rubbed time-
eroded beech and fingers intertwine
wrapped lovingly around the difference
which incites
tender researches
through our histories

glows transparent
burns surface-suffused
impassioned
as feeling coursing blood-dark through the heart
illumines
depth-charged thoughts which rise
skin-translucent

merges with muffled memories
of dark and murderous acts
- echoes
of confused complicity
glimpsed through childhood clarity
wide-eyed
down gathering perspectives
of white rapacious centuries
black hells
structured stark by whiteness until
devastations of darkness
imposed
silence
on plundered wastelands clean-stripped
vultured of the voiceless whispers
bone-bare
of latent songs of histories
whose ghost- caressed cadences
shimmer
and dream deep within your soul's
luminous profundities
- echoes
which resonate and underlie
our loving conversations.

The black silk velvet
of your skin
melts into darkness
marginless
in your deep doorway
where you stand
late-night-enveloped
and your smiles
incandescent with
the neon
whiteness of your teeth
flash a disembodied kiss
across the lamp-lit street
glimpsed as I look back and you
merge magicked spirited
away all outline swallowed
by surrounding shadows.

Structural Adjustment Blues

For Fredrick

When you came back
after the summer
trailing clouds of heat
exploding from
cement surfaces
white-hot with dust
swept on burning winds
whipping sand-scorched
along drained-white streets
and sultry shadows
of nights of Africa
perfumed and vengeful,
all your talk was of the ills
of structural adjustment
- enforced privatisations
abrupt closures
sudden deaths
mismanagement
corruption
emigrations
poverty
deterioration wide-
spread private anxiety
and no work to be had no
work anywhere to be found
- and your eyes
fresh from two years of absence
mirrored the decline
horrified
as Africa sinks
embattled
overwhelmed,
and
distraught
shocked with
the violence of transition
you shrank back in your skin
as if to emphasise

the distance between us,
no word
not one
affectionate word
passing the barrier
of your lips:
I grounded the shock
buffered the distress
submitted my hurt
to structural adjustments of the heart,
smashed the convoluted spirals
enmeshing maze-like to enshrine
the self-absorbed indulgences of pain,
adapted the structure
of my orchid dreams
tended delicate,
richly nurtured on
lush memories grown
exotic with longing
through the hot-house summer
of your absence,
turned on them
the violence of compassion
and, appalled
by the harsh force of your stories,
got practical.

Songs from the Twilight Zone of Your Absence

for Cyprian Katongo

The night you left
time changed
and shrank
and winter
overwhelmed

pale sunlit
golden bright
autumnal
afternoons
night-enforced
diminished
dwindled down
to darkness

after you left
night fell
at five
and blackness
overwhelmed

and I
blighted
stricken
past tears
crept cold
to bed
all inhospitable

where I
warmed the wildness
of my grief's
frozen wastelands'
wilderness

with memories
times of love

when lulled by your caresses
the sun-enraptured meadow
of my body passion-drenched
lay indolent extended
basking in abandonment
opened flowered and flourished in
dream-fulfilled realities
of your presence
everynight

where I
filled the wilderness
of my grief's
empty wastelands'
loneliness

with memories
times of love

when lulled by soft cadences
of your voice I wandered through
harmonious hours of talk
dappled green with orchard light
or shared over food and wine
candle-lit by the brilliance
of your smile – rites illumined
by your presence
everyday

where I
soothed the wildness
of my grief's
aching wastelands'
painfulness

with memories
times of love

when we went adventuring
exuberant with freedom
arrow-sped down motorways
danced down undulating lanes
recovered dreams of landscapes
half-forgotten childhood shapes
clear rainbowed through the prism
of your presence
everywhere

after you left
and I
wounded
rent
survived
the hurt
of distancing

slowly
here in the twilight zone
I rekindle
our happiness
lonely
here in the twilight zone
of your absence.

OF POETRY, DANCE AND MUSIC

The White Heat of Poetry I

Intensity
is my only talent
- a two-edged weapon
at the best of times -
that's why the white heat
of poetry
suits me so perfectly
when words coalesce
in concentration
experience merged
moulded molten
by the flux of feeling
into pure meaning
captured energy
held taut in tension
brief explosion
structured into metre
burnt-out falling star
expressing densely
all I want to say.

The White Heat of Poetry II

Poetry is my undoing
these days I can't think
of anything else
get daily more abstracted
I'm too hazy
even
to eat
let alone to work.

Prosers have to be more or less
intelligible
quite articulate
with sequential narrative
I'm too crazy -
no one
expects
poetry to be sane.

Even the mere idea of prose
writing articles
perhaps a novel
fills me with utter horror
I'm too lazy
by far -
my God
the thought of all those words!

A character heroic in
stature is needed
to be prosaic
ardent and keen in research
it's so easy
just to
daydream
doodling idly in verse.

You can get away with much more
writing poetry
punctuation rhyme
metre are matters of choice
sublime breezy
cheek of
free verse
on the loose from the rules.

What seems quite inspirational
in poetry looks
utterly impious
in prose – my subject matter
is too sleazy
sexy
and stark
has to be veiled in verse.

Dancer

For Darryl

Angels are everywhere
and materialise
intra-dimensional

but you are the angel of violence

and explode
exultant
through the senses

whose vibrant body bears
tensioned in its sinews
encoded memories
branded
lashed
upon the structure of its cells
of unspeakable cruelties
of whips
of chains
of voiceless screams
which echo and pulsate
with anguished energy

which you translate
into an avenging beauty
whose proud severity
contains
transcends
intensities of pain
which tear
and rend
wild
across the heart strings
and yet exhilarate.

Afro-Caribbean Night at the Dance Exchange

For my dear friend, Mafuta Sam, dancer extraordinaire and Samba Queen of Great Britain 1995-1996 – my enthusiastic accomplice in late-night dancing.
- and in appreciative memory of the fabulous dancers and drummers of Kokuma Afro-Caribbean Dance Theatre who lit up our Tuesday nights with their joyful exuberance in the early 90's.

Saché right down
to the Dance-Exchange -
at 7.15 on Tuesday night.
If you're running on empty
and luck's way out of sight,
Kokuma will still waft you
as high as a kite.

So leave your worries
well outside the door -
there's no time for grief and sorrow
on the dancing floor.

Da da di da da di da da da
Stick your bum out.
Shake your boobs.
You've gotta try the Kokuma
cure for the blues.
It's breathless
it's exhilarating
it's cheaper than drugs
and stronger than booze.

Wear something loose
with plenty of leeway
for pelvic gyrations and floor-level plier.
You'll feel more relaxed
in sufficient elasticity
to show off your assets
in full mobility.

So chuck your shoes off
just inside the door -
you don't need shoes and socks
on the dancing floor.

Da da di da da di da da da
Stick your bum out.
Shake your boobs.
You've gotta try the Kokuma
cure for the blues.
It's breathless
it's the latest craze
it's stronger than booze
and more purple than haze.

Don't waste your money
on Bacardi and coke.
You'll not only get hungover
but you'll be broke.
Who needs adverts for
exotic virtuality -
at the Dance Exchange there's
Afro-Caribbean sheer reality!

Shut the freezing cold fog and rain
right outside the door -
it's steaming – tropics hot
on the dancing floor.

Da da di da da di da da da
Stick your bum out.
Shake your boobs.
You've gotta try the Kokuma
cure for the blues.
It's breathless
it's exhilarating
it's cheaper than drugs
and stronger than booze.

If Senegal's your fancy
and you can't afford the flight,
just get down to the Dance Exchange
on Tuesday night.
Kokuma's dancers have all been there
and they'll be happy to share
that thrilling experience with you -
Senegalese costume, dance and flair.

Da da di da da di da da da
Faites saillir le po-po,
en avant la poitrine -
you've gotta try Kokuma's
dancing scene.
It's breathless
it's adieu – tristesse -
more ecstatic than ecstasy
more accessible than hash.

Shake off your Anglo-Saxon
inhibitions -
even puritans yield
to Kokuma's rhythms.

Leave your scrupulous rigidity
well outside the door,
and liquidise your spine
on the dancing floor.

Da da di da da di da da da
Stick your bum out.
Shake your boobs.
You've gotta try the Kokuma
cure for the blues.
It's breathless
it's rapturous
it's bang on the beat
- when the drummer starts to play
you'll be right up on your feet
because it's so irresistible
you just can't refuse -
more delirious than drugs
more subliminal than booze.

Trumpeter

For Jay Phelps, the brilliant jazz trumpeter

On the edge of harmony
on the edge of time
raw and shrill
the trumpet sears across memory
electric
gunshots ricochet across the room
staccato.
It's soaring punctuation
cut's through the drumbeats' rapid pulse
taut as high-tension cable
exhilarating
rapturously modulating
a sudden change of mood.
The phrasing liquifies, melodious and smooth
as sweet, dark wine flowing mellow
as mavrodaphne across the enthralled mind,
lusciously lyrical and tender,
a gentle nightscape silvered by the moon.

For you, Jay

and in memory of that notorious gig at Birmingham's
"Hare and Hounds" when I first heard you play.

Of course, you're instantly arrestable
you're so noticeable, so hard to ignore.
The police aren't known for their sense of humour,
mischievous playfulness, passion for jazz.
They sense you could start a public disorder
just with eight bars of delirious jazz.

In an age of bleak austerity
you're so lavish with virtuosity
so prodigal with creativity
so spendthrift with beauty and flair.

In an age of don't-rock-the-boat
mediocrity
you're so brilliantly off the scale.
At the sound of your trumpet
all the boats in the harbour
zip out to sea on a force-nine gale.

At a time when the jazz fraternity
rolled out of bed wearing yesterday's jeans
you were out there in a cool pastel suit
with lines as sharp as blades.

So yes, you're eminently arrestable
you're so harmonically way off-the-scale
you're so daringly empirical
so inspiringly lyrical
so deliciously far beyond the pale
just so outrageous, so anarchic
such an easy cop
you're so irresistibly, so irredeemably
right over the top.

To be brief -
forgive my temerity.
Just had to hear you again.

CONVERSATIONS WITH VLADIMIR MAYAKOVSKY

ON LOVE, LIFE, REVOLUTION, DEATH, TRANSLATION AND THE FUTURE TENSE

Introduction

I first came across the poems of the Russian writer, Vladimir Mayakovsky, (19 July 1893 – 14 April 1930) in 1997 and was immediately struck by his palpable confidence and energy bouncing off the pages expressed in dramatic exaggeration, graphic imagery and surreal effects and by his use of colloquial, street language and his playful positioning of words, which were apparently scattered across the pages sometimes. Even in translation, notoriously difficult for poetry, the man's vitality in the original writing was unmistakable. I had a lot of fun attempting to imitate some of the aspects of his flamboyant style in the conversations and I even noticed a slight influence on other things I was writing at the time. Then I became busy with other things and forgot about Mayakovsky for upwards of twenty years. In 2020 I suddenly, for no particular reason, started thinking about him again and remembering how impressed I'd been by his work so I got out his poems and also looked at one or two other translations and several commentaries on his extraordinary life lived out so passionately through one of the most extreme and dangerous periods of history, which I'd known nothing about before. It was like meeting up with a very old friend after a long absence and catching up with everything that had happened in their life in the meantime. As before he leapt off the page and commanded my complete attention and of course I had lots of questions. Hence the set of further conversations.

Mayakovsky was born in Georgia of a Cossack father and a Ukrainian mother. He later regarded Georgia as a lost paradise because of its great beauty. His father died suddenly in 1906 when Vladimir was thirteen and his mother sold up and moved the family – Vladimir and his two sisters – to Moscow. By the age of sixteen he was already a Bolshevik activist and in 1909 was sent to prison for seven months for helping to free some women prisoners, and it was in prison that he first began writing verse. Precocious and passionate, he was truly a child of the revolution already politically active in his teens and serving a political and revolutionary apprenticeship, as it were, in the years leading up to 1917. After prison he continued writing poetry and in 1911, aged 18, he entered Moscow Art School where he met another student, David Burlyuk, with whom he founded a branch of the new Futurist Movement devoted to freeing the arts from academic traditions, and they began giving anarchic public readings of their work at which they dressed up and behaved outrageously, culminating in 1913 with a riotous Russian tour of seventeen cities. As a result of clashes with the police in various places, he and Burlyuk were expelled from the Art School in 1914. Although he remained true to the spirit of the Revolution throughout his life, he was never a party member and his relations with the state remained unstable and later turbulent mainly because of his individualistic temperament and love of artistic freedom.

After college Mayakovsky worked for various journals and newspapers, contributing articles and poems. In 1915 he met a married couple, Osip and Lilya Brik. The Briks had been married several years and had already decided never to have children and to end their sexual relations but had agreed a pact whereby they would always stay together and would practice a policy of free love, both having other sexual partners without jealousy or rancour. Mayakovsky fell madly in love with Lilya on their first meeting and dedicated his just-finished long poem, "A Cloud in Trousers", to her. This poem, both a love poem and an explanation of his political ideas, was to become one of his most famous works. It seems likely that she did not reciprocate his love but was flattered by his attention and totally obsessed by the idea of becoming his muse. As she put it herself, she immediately knew that he was a genius, but she didn't like him – he was too loud, rough-mannered and uncouth and everybody stared at him because he was so tall. So there was obsession on both sides from the beginning, but their obsessions didn't fit. Osip welcomed him enthusiastically into their lives and they became close friends with Osip acting as his publisher. In 1918 Mayakovsky moved in with them and they lived together until his death. Mayakovsky was never happy or fulfilled by their love affair and their sexual relationship ended in 1923 after which they both had a series of affairs with other people. In spite of the unsatisfactory nature of the love affair between Vladimir and Lilya, the threesome arrangement was probably advantageous to all three of them. Vladimir and Osip maintained a stimulating and productive working and intellectual partnership and a lifelong friendship. Vladimir had the advantage of Osip's organisational abilities in the publishing and selling of his poems and other writings while Osip took inspiration from the poet's brilliance and energy. Because of Mayakovsy's great fame and reputation the Briks were able to set up a thriving artistic salon which was frequented by the most famous writers and artists of the time, and Lilya achieved the fame she craved as his muse and the dedicatee of his most famous love poems. Living with the Briks brought a kind of stability into Vladimir's life which had suffered from the extreme emotional instability of his temperament and the practical difficulties of his hand-to-mouth existence as a young artist establishing himself during a period of unprecedented shortages due to the defeat of the Imperial Russian Army towards the end of the First World War and the civil war during The Revolution which followed, when many Russians starved to death.

The ten years from 1917 to 1927 show the extraordinary intensity of his working life and the immense diversity of his gifts and interests. During these years a constant stream of poems flowed from his pen – love poems, political poems, poems for children as well as a number of satirical plays, essays on political subjects, the aesthetics of poetry and his travels abroad, and articles for various journals and newspapers. He edited several journals, some on futurism and the journal of the Left Art Front which examined the ideology and practice of leftist art. He produced and acted in his own plays as well as a number of films and carried out numerous tours of lectures and poetry readings. His public appearances were legendary because of his powerful and expressive voice which was said to be capable of overpowering any amount of heckling. From 1919 he worked for ROSTA, The State Telegraph Agency, designing and producing thousands of posters aimed at informing the proletariat of current events and he went on to produce publicity posters for many industrial companies, thus making use of his art training in his graphic work which was ultra modern in style and as intense and powerful as his writing.

In the years up to 1927 Mayakovsky's fame and popularity as poet of the Revolution resulted in him having more freedom than usual to travel abroad, and he visited Germany,

England, Latvia, France, Mexico and the USA. In 1925 he stayed in New York for three months and renewed his friendship with David Burlyuk who was by then living in America. He also met Yelizaveta Zibert, a Russian emigrée who had fled from Russia with the aid of an Englishman whom she later married. She and Mayakovsky fell deeply in love and had an affair throughout the three months which they kept secret. The following year she gave birth to their daughter, Patricia, whom Mayakovsky saw once in 1928 when he managed to get to France to meet them on holiday in Nice. Patricia spent her life in New York where she became a writer and professor of Philosophy, but travelled to Russia in 1991 to trace her roots, after which she adopted her father's name. She had married a man called Thompson and had a son who accompanied her to Russia.

After 1928 Mayakovsky's relations with the state rapidly deteriorated. His two satirical plays "The Bedbug" (1929) and "The Bathhouse" (1930) were strongly criticised by the Association of Proletarian Writers because they made mock of the growing bureaucracy and its attempts to limit artistic freedom. His exhibition "20 years of Work" was ignored by Stalin and other state dignitaries and he was booed at a couple of lecture appearances in early 1930. In spite of his fame, success and fearless criticism of the bureaucracy he seems to have been unduly distressed by the various rejections of his latest work. He was also finding it much more difficult to travel abroad because his applications for visas were suddenly being refused. His seemingly ever more desperate attempts to find someone to marry were also constantly ending in failure, especially as he seemed to fall usually for married women. He had high hopes of marrying a beautiful Russian emigrée working as a model whom he had met in Paris in 1928, who understandably had deep doubts about returning to Russia where she would most likely have been in danger. His plans to go to Paris in 1930 to marry her and bring her back to Russia were dashed when he was refused a visa. There were rumours that Lilya had manipulated this refusal through contacts she and Osip had in the secret police. He then had a brief affair with a young actress, Nora Polonskaya, but she refused to leave her husband in spite of Vladimir begging her to do so. In the spring of 1930 Osip and Lilya went abroad for weeks on an extended trip. On the morning of 4th April 1930, after a row with Nora the previous evening, he shot himself. Having just left his office and hearing the shot, she rushed back in only to find him lying dead on the floor.

He had probably often rehearsed his suicide in his mind, having owned a pistol ever since adolescence. He apparently talked about it sometimes to friends and as early as 1915 in the prologue to his long poem "The Backbone Flute" he writes:-

"I contemplate -
                    so often -
ending my days
with the full stop of a bullet.
This evening,
                    for all of you -
                                        just in case -
I am giving a farewell concert."

The mirror image of the manic intensity of much of his working and emotional life – the opposite end of the spectrum – was deep bouts of depression which overwhelmed him from time to time. Although none of the commentaries mention it, I am sure now he would be diagnosed as having a manic-depressive personality – not to the point of being mentally ill but as characterised by his extreme emotional instability and violent mood swings, his ability to work all night for days on end and the volatility and depth of his passions. The commentaries were mostly written before the bi-polar syndrome began to be seen as a distinct personality type merging into mental illness at its most extreme.

Endless rumours circulated about his death and the possibility it was murder disguised as suicide. His note – "To all of you. I die, but don't blame anyone for it, and please do not gossip. Mother, sisters, comrades, forgive me – this is not a good method, but there is no other way out for me." – was disputed but felt to be authentic after much research decades later. His funeral three days later was attended by 150,000 mourners, surpassed only by the numbers at the funerals of Lenin and Stalin. Several years after his death, his reputation as the greatest poet of the Revolution was re-instated after a letter to Stalin requesting this from Lilya Brik. Osip left Lilya shortly after Vladimir's death and lived with his secretary. After Osip's death a few years later, Lilya married twice more and survived well into her eighties, still insisting on describing herself as "Mayakovsky's widow."

Conversations with Vladimir Mayakovsky
– on love, life, revolution, death, translation and the future tense.

I don't know about clouds in trousers,
Mayakovsky,
- personally I prefer something
more fleshly and corporeal
behind the male zip -
but I remember calculating
- I must have been six or seven at the time -
that in the year 2000 I'd be sixty
and I still remember like it's this morning
the elation of pure genius
in front of a mind-boggling discovery,
and I still am now that flash of genius
containing all my ages,
energy soaring and sky-diving
smashing through tensed surfaces
into depths of mood darkness,
dancing all night intoxicated
with fluent-black-hands-going-beautifully-berserk-
on-those-drums-in-ecstasy rhythm
and saxophones screaming through the heart,
lusting after young men with sinuous hips
before the paunch and male menopausal angst
take over at forty.
Being a women I'm through that stage
- zooming way out through the stratosphere
into outer space of post-pausal energy
age-defying soars my fervent soul -
playing myself like the gypsy's clarinet
on the third day of non-stop celebration
at some mountain wedding in Epiros when
only booze and elation keep him
on his feet this side of exhaustion,
working on the wild side of sane
in the business centre
where I'm a liability
but they can't fire me just hire me

because I am a mercenary
for use in an emergency
when I weave my spells
and leave.

If you were writing now, Mayakovsky,
you'd be rapping like crazy
with those hot rhythms
in some steamy club
rapping in Russian
and perhaps you are
somewhere.

I don't think you're well-served
by your translator, Mayakovsky,
or maybe your Russian is
non-transmutable
non-catalytic outside its culture.

Having forgotten what Russian
I painfully learnt
--- dying of thirst in the desert
during that psychotic year
under the shrieking blue skies
of pitiless Athena
at the Soviet Institute
in the posh part
just round the bend from Syntagma
catering to the artistic elite
and as elites go, and they did,
were they snooty?
or was I just too mad
to take part?
a couple of years
before the colonels
closed it down
and that was the end
of that particular bit
of history
political
and personal, ---
I can't really be sure.

But I suspect that they've made a hash
of the translation and it's pure trash
- could probably be some American academical
of the post-cold-war era waxing horribly lyrical
- the language is just so weird.
Anyone else would be too afeard
to attempt to force any kind of restriction
on your melodramatic love-struck affliction,
to coerce your baneful futurist cursification
straight into strainful post-modernist versification,
or to think for a moment of trying to stop
you from going absolutely over the top,
Mayakovsky.

Man, how could they do it to you?
A cloud in Y-fronts, for God's sake!
Or is it a joke
that fails to survive
the two-way Atlantic crossing
plus a quick dip in Baltic ice
at sub-zero minus forty?

Did you actually crave
translation
even at this price
internationalisation
at the cost of unspeakable rhymes
eternalisation
beyond the confines of your times?

Is it in fact you translating in another life
taking the transatlantic mick?
Did you have a sense of humour?
- it's not that clear from your poem – or
is it a reincarnated
still vicious Maria getting in the final kick?

If you were writing now, Mayakovsky,
you'd be rapping like crazy
with those hot rhythms
in some steamy club
and perhaps you are
somewhere
because, man, that's where
the revolution is these days.

They tell me, Mayakovsky,
you're a revolutionary
--- I use the present tense advisedly -
revolutionaries never die
merely evaporate
into other lives
drifting down the centuries
and you are
they are still around
even in this smug - besotted
just-about-still-sceptred isle
in the very late twentieth century
and elsewhere they abound
in much greater numbers.
Maybe they have clouds in their trousers
- revolutionaries tend to have clouds
secreted somewhere about their persons
in their heads
suspending their dreams
on billowing white silk parachutes
although the fingers on the trigger
and the fingers that weld
the wires to the fuse
tend to be more material
as does the shrapnel
and the severed limbs
of those who take the full blast
in their bodies
and students in countless squares
stand immaterialised by passion
until the bullets' hail
rips through their bodies
and they know they're flesh.

For in most parts of the world
where it's difficult to afford
the luxury of reading
people still think history exists
and want to be making it
and want to be part of it
so revolutions are bloody
and bitterly fought.

So Fuk-u-yamerica!
What a shame you didn't realise
that when at last all the enemies
had fallen into the hiatus
between the final end of history
and the start of a new world order
that the rest of us can visualise,
you alone remain as focus for
all our loathing and have finally
attained most-hated-nation status.

Otherwise, here,
paradoxically,
politics of the belly
and the mortgage rule,
along with democracy
of course,
OK?

Nevertheless, Mayakosky,
as you surely know,
revolutionaries
are still around now even here.
We're assailing the barricades
in board rooms these days,
flinging ourselves at the platform
where Rio Tinto Zinc
ranges its non-executive directors
- and God knows in their arrogance
they're as unassailable as tanks -
shrieking abuse at the ranks of Giordanos
before the heavies manhandle us to the floor,
hanging effigies on Shell petrol stations
- in Nigeria, of course,
they are doing it for real
and wherever the front line is
and the bravest of the brave.
We have no delusions
- we don't over-estimate our position
way back in the rearguard.

Nevertheless,
as we constantly tell
passers-by who abuse us,
company headquarters are not in Lagos
and the sepulchral ranks of grey men
crumbling to dust in the too bright light of day
with a sprinkling of women masked in make-up
in sharp suits and dagger-high heels
- she isn't grey like they are
she's had to fight her way in too
for her this is a kind of victory -
the grey ones are not in Bougainville
they're right here
among us
and they're our bit
- tangible, tactile, corporeal -
our assailable bit
of the global enemy.

And no doubt
we still have clouds
in our heads.

I realise, Mayakovsky,
that suggesting humility
is a lost cause with you,
but believe me you'll need some work
on your street credibility
- crucifying yourself nightly
on stage in the name of J.C.
just isn't in these days.
Man, you need to get cool
to join the revolution now.

The arrogant style and sinuous hips
are still in fashion – some things never change.
These days they're swinging on high harnessed to
some tree-top over the next by-pass site.

Revolutionaries now are practical
and down to earth, choosing limited goals.
No one now expects the second coming
except the Americans who think they
are its collective manifestation.
Elsewhere change is seen as a long process
so you may as well enjoy the journey.
So here's hoping that on the other side
of Lethe you found yourself a short course
in survival for the next time around.

And by the way,
what's the point of
pursuing Maria
so vociferously?
Revolutionaries should be
self-disciplined and focussed
right on the business in hand.
They don't need to tempt trouble
in the form of lyric verse
and falling madly in love
with difficult women.

Or was Maria getting her own back?
Was it your bad behaviour? – Nadezhda
doesn't seem to think much of your lousy manners -
were you too obsessed to take 'no' for an answer?
Did love in fact have anything to do with it?

Further Conversations with Vladimir Mayakovsky

Whatever happened to you,
Vladimir? You might have left
a more explicit note.
Did you really pull the trigger,
Volodya, how could you be so crazy?
You've left us puzzled and bereft -
or did some jealous husband
or malevolent uncle Jo
pay a hit-man to top you,
ending your life of passion
in the usual Soviet fashion?
You owe it to your fans -
what really happened, Vol?
No gossip, we promise -
we're just so curious to know.

Did your meteor spirit
reach its zenith far too early,
did you sense its imminent burn-out,
anguished loss of Icaros impetus
and melting in despair plunge seaward?

Had you done it all by twenty,
facing only endless ennui,
serial amours by thirty
and apparatchik propaganda?
Was your fate to effervesce
and fade?

Frustrated by futile affairs,
fed-up with flighty married women
- didn't you notice they were married to richer men than you, like Osip?
far less exciting, far less irresistibly alluring
but better-heeled than you – no more fur coats -
enmeshed and smothered
by Lilya's pitiless
manipulations,
trapped, caught by cancelled visas
could you find no way out? -
but a sensational last performance
in your inimitable dramatic style?
--- BANG --- far too final for a futurist!

Did you see the light
in a blinding flash?
Did it finally click that brittle Lilya Brik
wasn't at all what she seemed to be? ---
the glamorous muse? --- no
the generous patroness? --- no
a wily smooth operator? --- yes
lusting after power and influence,
blood-sucking your energy,
merchandising your genius,
capitalising on your naïve youth,
selling the sultry explosive charm
of your anarchic presence.

Surely moody Polonskaya
sulking off homeward after yet
another pointless set -
to wasn't worth a bullet
through the heart?

Surely you could see a future
with all your brilliance and your fame,
or were you so drugged up on youth,
was reaching forty so passé
so graceless and uncouth
so "grey – hairs – in – the – soul"
just so yesterday?
You are a futurist, aren't you?
For God's sake, had life so lost it's sense,
were you so washed up in limbo,
without a future or a present tense?

Or was your future closing in?
Did your patron, uncle Joseph,
turning nasty, start to cramp your style,
at thirty-six to hem you in with rules?
Was it bitter disillusion
- no present, no future vision?
Was the revolution turning grey,
vitality ebbing, freedom vanishing away?

If only you'd been more patient,
had you waited for a while,
you might have found a future
in the New World with your daughter,
Patricia, enjoyed the present
of her childhood, with your past found
peaceful reconciliation.
Patricia would have taught you better balance
shared your highs, consoled your lows,
with a steadying hand contained your manic vertigo.
You might have learnt to savour less impetuous,
long-enduring, gentler
forms of love and found new
inspiration late-ripening
with autumnal, calm reflection
on the unexpected richness
of multi-faceted old age.

Patricia knew what patience was.
She waited till perestroika
then took her chance and ventured east
flew to Russia at sixty-five
- she sure was not going to spend her life
in one of uncle Joseph's
summer camps in Siberia -
she had her own career, her books,
her life in academia,
prof. of philosophy, her family -
but she still craved to chase your ghost,
the father she saw once, aged two.
She kept your portrait in her study
at the centre of her life -
your moody sultry dark good looks
still dominate the room.
In memory of you
she took your name, Yelena
Vladimirovna Mayakovskaya.
That was a love worth waiting for
if love was really your desire.

Where's the revolution now?
- you may well ask, Vol.
Dead in Russia along with most revolutionaries
- there are still valiant individuals
risking all by speaking out.
Putin favours Stalin's methods,
no clouds about him – except of nerve gas.
His chosen weapon is silent, secret, deadly poison.
You might, they might not agree
but your heirs are Pussy Riot
glamorous, flamboyant girl band -
yes, Vol, I did say "girl band" -
women now don't want to be muses
don't want to be passive
they demand to be
part of the action
like Pussy Riot doing it for real -
loud, scandalous, transgressive
with their illegal pop-up shows
tumultuous
in squares and churches
when they're not in gaol.

Americans dream of total immunity
from science, climate change, pandemic disease,
economic meltdown, Wall Street crashes and refugees
- everything except money in Trump's America.
They're irrelevant now.

The UK's had it -
hardly worth a mention.
Floundering, flooded by think tanks
- they're the right – wing menace now -
drifting off Europe's northern margin.
Boris Johnson's lost the rudder -
silly bugger!
We're irrelevant now.

Europe's still got it together
largely free from lethal tyrants
united, civilised, engaged.
Hopefully they have a future.

Rebels do still exist
in the Middle East, around China.
Thousands have died in Syria, Libya and Iraq
"supported" by the West
achieving material devastation
political social fragmentation,
still in thrall to tribal structures
and religion.
After the bloodstained Arab Spring
summer, autumn, winter keep passing
but the blood flows still unquenched,
the final outcome's still unsure.
Black people everywhere demand justice
fight on stoically determined
their lives will matter on their own terms.
They are the revolution now.
Then there's Extinction Rebellion
set up and run by children
- sick of adult inaction -
to save the future.
If there is one, they are it -
they should take ownership.

Because, Volodya –

The big question now is
whether the future tense itself exists -
for humanity, for the world
even for the universe.
Are we all bound for cosmic burn-out?
How would you face up to that one,
Vladimir,
in your life or in your art?
Would you have a different answer now
or the same one ------
A BULLET THROUGH THE HEART?

Index of Poems

BV - #0059 - 190422 - C0 - 297/210/9 - PB - 9781914424489 - Matt Lamination